MW01144696

LIFE'S LESSONS

Memoirs of Sex & Lies, Love & Death

For & By
Arthur A Jennings
COPYRIGHT 2015
Czar Struck LLC.

This is autobiographical in nature. This is the work of one man's reflection of his own life. All the names that are questionable have been omitted, changed or mentioned in a positive manner. The contents of this work including, but not limited to, the accuracy of events, people and places depicted as well as opinions expressed are nostalgic and solely the responsibility of the author and his life experiences.

LIFE'S LESSONS: MEMOIRS OF SEX & LIES, LOVE & DEATH

Copyright © 2015 by Arthur A Jennings

First Edition Published by
Czar Struck LLC
P O Box 2254
Center, TX 75935
1-888-775-1567

No part of this book may be reproduced or transmitted in any form or by any means, electronic or mechanical, including photocopying, recording or by any information storage and retrieval system without permission in writing from the author.

All Rights Reserved
ISBN: 1512334936
ISBN 13: 9781512334937

Printed in the United States of America

My Deepest Appreciation…

First goes to my unwavering wife, Jessie, whom I love uncon-ditionally. Thank you for not judging me for my somber past, but allowing me to liberate myself in the writings of my darkest nature. Special thanks go out to Ron, aka Adolphus Herndon of Czar Struck LLC for believing in me and helping make my literary legacy a reality. Without you, this would remain just a dream. I'd also like to thank artist Diane L. Drashner for allowing her beautiful and commemorative work to be the feature cover.

LIFE'S LESSONS

Memoirs of Sex & Lies, Love & Death

Arthur A Jennings

FOREWORD

Life's Lessons is an honest account of the things we least like to talk about, the stains we keep covered up for years after The Incident. With a fluid and unapologetic style of storytelling, Art gives his audience permission to say what they really mean, feel and think, however late in life. His off-color humor and revelation of the best and worst moments of his life paint an unrivaled picture of human existence.

To be sure, Art's writings are not for the timid, happy-ending kind of reader. In Chapter 2 of Part One, "Sex and Lies," Art describes "a well-hidden sexual underground" or club frequented by his stepfather, an apparent stepping stone into the depths of emotional damage and a future of dysfunctional relationships. Art's almost accidental tendency toward sexual promiscuity follows him into the military, resulting in a tangled "family" of hurt individuals around the world. In this story, some wounds never heal.

But being a hard worker and a man of accomplished wit — though the reader will find a shameless fart joke in his text — Art finds some successes in his life, not limited to his artistic endeavors and fishing trips in Alaska. Art's creativity pays off in the military, booting a bad battalion executive commander, essentially, with a "field sanitation" class, and his determination to do right after doing so much wrong eventually wins him back the love of his life, however fractured that love has been. "[She] meant everything to me and I vowed that if I had to spend every waking moment of every day for the rest of my life in therapy, I would not stray," he writes in Chapter 9 of Part Two, "Love and Death."

For readers who like a chronological storyline, getting used to the jumps and flashbacks and references in Art's writings will require an adjustment. All Art's anecdotes are punctuated with self-insight — even if there are no answers — and sometimes may seem disjointed. But isn't that the way people tend to tell long stories about their lives anyway?

Having interviewed the author prior to his death, I can say for sure that Arthur Allen Jennings led an interesting life, worthy of publication. In his memoirs, perhaps we can find the courage to uncover the stains in our lives sooner rather than later.

— Caitlin Skvorc

This book is dedicated to...
All the many people who were victims and casualties as a result of my lies of infidelity; be it wives, past lovers, my children and friends. The pains I have inflicted upon you has returned to its source tenfold.

PROLOGUE: PART I

I have felt the gentle winds and soft rain of fall on my face. My winter approaches. Fall's mist has risen and the dark cold is upon me. A sense of my past overwhelms me, like a warm breeze on a cold day. There is no fear, just a sense of awareness.

I have died a thousand deaths, by fire, water, ice, gravity and suffocation; by accident, man-made, animal and my suicide; war and peace, disease, even my own imagination while insane. We are all born and we all die, I can faintly remember most of those passing.

My lives have seen deserts turn to swamps, to forests, to grasslands and back to deserts, monuments go up and empires crumble, two thousand times. I have lived in each with luster.

I have crushed a shrew and split a mammoth and had the same done to me. I fear height, water, beasts; trust women but not men and embrace the dark.

One thousand and one, life has been hard. Welcomed death will come easy and with relish. I do not fear this death, rather I will embrace it. I wonder what the next life will bring but don't care. There will be another. My present "ME" shall become an obscure enigma to ancestors yet to be conceived.

My sentient being is but symbiont to this mass and will be recycled, I shall return as another; from the One.

Relax everyone. Dying is easy; I'm guessing. It's living that's a bitch; I'm sure of that.

PROLOGUE: PART II

Ok, so I am an atheist. But on the other hand, I believe religion is good for mankind. I would defend, to the death, mankind's right to worship any god they wish in almost any way they wish. I get angry at the anti-religion group railing against the cross or expression of religion in public places. What are they afraid of? I really would go out of my way to insult atheists who attempt to block any worship or symbolism.

I have seen the other side and whether you are spiritual or a non-believer, it's the same end. One path just has more rules and a few opportunists interjecting themselves into our life and taking advantage of humankind's fears and doubts. I, of course, am not trying to become one of them. I am writing my story because I have found peace in what has happened to me. As an atheist, I would be glad to go to your church and hold your hand while you pray.

LIFE'S LESSONS

Memoirs of Sex & Lies, Love & Death

PART I

SEX & LIES

1

IN THE BEGINNING

"**S**hadows from the past" has been used many times when writing of our memories. I'm sure by now, that expression must be worn out. Yet, I wish I had thought of it and it had never been used before. I like it. I have an extensive and good memory and my own personal shadows are very bold and deep. I can drift back to a time in my past that stands out and engrossed myself not only in the memory of that moment, but I can feel the atmosphere, be it a hot and humid day, cold and rainy or my favorite, a warm breeze on the ocean. Especially bad is the heat and humidity of the jungle. With the good though, comes the bad. I can also relive some of the embarrassing feelings when I think of things I have done that I should have not.

This is just part of my story. It was written during moments of clarity from June 2012 to June 2014. This time was given to me by a doctor and a hospital full of wonderful and dedicated people in Albany, Oregon when a lung collapsed in June 2012. I was given up for dead but the powers that be decided to allow an experimental mercy operation, more for the purpose of medical research I would guess. It worked and the project is going well I hear.

Some say my writing doesn't say enough, some say it says too much. My problem is that I remember everything from 1945 to present. That's a lot to recall and write about. I can't always put everything in order but remembering everything is a curse. Should I tell you how good it felt every time I took a piss or how I felt at the birth of each of my children, grandchildren and newly discovered great-grandchildren?

As my demise approaches, moments in my waiting time appear. At times a sense of calm sweeps over me and, with my story in front of me, I contemplate about past friends.

"Where are they now? Do they still live?"

It saddens me when I hear of the death of someone from my past. Not just my family but friends and people that I just knew of. Thinking of the things that I have experienced in the recent past, why do I still fear death? I should trust what I have seen and felt; I know it to be true that something is waiting for me on the other side. Why should the break with life be so complete? I may return as my mother has returned to me. I'll let you know in a subtle way.

When I was a teenager, my mother gave me the responsibility of cooking for the family. She and my stepfather both worked full time and she said it was necessary to keep her away from that duty. One of the first things she taught me was how to fry potatoes. When she was growing up, many times, all her family had to eat was a bag of potatoes and my grandmother had to be a good cook to satisfy so many mouths.

"Use a hot pan, plenty of bacon and fat, and too many onions. Always mix completely and listen for the crackle," she instructed.

Mom tried to teach me to use cast iron as that is all they had when she was young. Now we have the super slick Teflon. I know how to use cast iron and it is probably better but Teflon is so much easier. The crackle comes when the potatoes are just the right color to turn. After 40 more years of practice I finely got it right. Today, my family will tell you that my breakfast fried potatoes will bring tears to your eyes.

If I were a philosopher I could use the lesson of listening to the crackle and apply it to life's learning paths. But, I missed that chapter and late in life I realize I had lacked the patience to listen enough. I believe I must have missed a lot. I implore all who read this to learn to listen to the crackle; listen to others and stop talking about yourself so much; you know who you are.

Now that I near my end, I confess that I suffered from self-worship for much of my life; perhaps a mild form of narcissism. I should have been worshiping those patient enough to listen to me. I can truly say that my life has been eventful, interesting, exciting, and yes, meaningful. I must interject that I did make some poor choices that I am not proud in any way, shape or form.

Although previously mentioned, I do realize that I am not suffering from a full blown narcissistic personality disorder. However, for most of my adult years I have noticed that I always seemed to get conversations centered on me. To others, that must be very irritating.

One thing that contributed to my concern about this matter of narcissism is that I have been working on my book from only one computer. It was new when they brought it to me when I was in ICU in June 2012. Now, many years later, the keys are warn and hard to read. Is it not ironic that the letter

"I" is completely unreadable from its use? My story is not worthy of a novel but being a good storyteller I bet I can get a chuckle or two.

2

GROWING PAINS

I was born into this life on August 5, 1943 on a very hot day. I know that because I was there and in Hillsboro, Oregon, it is always hot in August. My mind can easily drift back and feel that Willamette Valley heat.

My mother was only seventeen. Think about that: seventeen. She was in the hospital twenty hours. Throughout my life, instead of celebrating my birthday the way most would, I would call her on the 5th of August. I would thank her for bearing the pain of childbirth and further, apologize for the pain I may have caused her while she raised me to be the man I was, at least the good part of me.

The hospital where I was born no longer exists. My father was listed on my birth certificate as a cannery worker and he was 43-years-old. I was 43 in 1986 and I remember it well, but, I can't imagine being married to a 17-year-old at that stage of my life. My mother and father were married in Stevensan, Washington, in the county of Skamania on the 4th day of September, 1942. Her mother and father were both there. When they married, my mother was just sixteen and my father was forty-two. I have never remembered my father in any way. I find that strange in that I remember so much of my life's experiences.

My mother's family was large, about eight kids along with my grandmother and grandfather. She told me many stories of how they survived in the hills around Provo, Utah. The family was able to get fresh meat without money or effort twice a year when the sheep herders moved their animals to seasonal pastures. Animals would tumble from their trails and die from the fall. As they were of no further use to the herders, they welcomed the meat. Eventually, as the family grew and matured, they began traveling up and down the West Coast picking crops.

If you watch the movie *The Grapes of Wrath* you are watching a mirror image of their way of life. I can imagine mom married to get away from that way of life but she never told me that. Many of my aunts and uncles and even my mother would return to picking crops when they needed some extra cash. I can remember being with several of them picking hops for the beer market somewhere in Oregon when I was about four.

They had to take me to the fields and to make me be good they would bribe me with fudge bars at the end of the day, my favorite at the time. I remember they only cost a nickel and I had no use for money so I elected for the cold stuff. Even as late as the mid 50's I remember going with mom to live in a migrant camp to pick strawberries and beans. She was just trying to earn extra money and she was a good picker. I was about 13 or 14 and spent most of my time just missing my first love, Jessie. I was never good at picking anything.

My mother often said that I was a difficult child to raise in my first four years. When she wanted to tell others of my antics and embarrass me a little, she would relate a time when she chased me out of the house as I was trying to escape a spanking. Luckily it was a quiet neighborhood as she said I ran into the street and began to taunt her to come get me. Can you imagine my defiance as I had been told to stay out of the street and thinking it was a safe escape, she would not follow?

She said she had stopped, as there was no traffic and she wanted to see what my next move was. When she started toward me, she said I reached into my diaper and threw a turd at her. She said everyone was laughing so hard that it was hard to give me the spanking I deserved but I did not escape that. In those days, about 1946-47, there were steel rings cemented into the street curbs of some of the old neighborhoods in Portland Oregon. They were for tying horses before cars. After the street incident, my mother told me she gave me the talk and that those rings were for tying bad children so they would stay out of the street. I do not remember the incident but I do remember the numerous times my mother would use the story to get a few laughs from others.

I did a lot of traveling as a preschooler. I remember trips to Utah to visit my grandmother. I also remember trips with my uncles; I think they were acting as baby sitters. There were also stays with aunts and uncles at various mining camps in Utah, Idaho, Montana and Nevada. Many of my uncles were miners. I recall one dying from black lung disease. Another, my favorite uncle, was killed in the Sunshine Mine Disaster in 1972.

I do remember B29 Bombers and blimps flying along the Oregon coast in my early years in Lincoln City. My first grade teacher was Mrs. Hendricks. I had to get up in front of the class and recite the alphabet and we took turns counting to 100. I attended grades one through five at Delake Grade School. The boys would play *Cowboys and Indians* and the girls would play nurse and fix our wounds. The big brick house of learning building now looks to be some kind of administration building.

When I was old enough, my mother let me walk or ride my bike to school. There was a Dairy Gold dairy products business a block or so from the school and I could stop in on the way home and buy a soft ice cream cone for 5 cents. After about the 5th grade, school was a mess. I became one of those who hung back socially and academically. I did not have enough credits to graduate from high school with my class so I joined the Army when I was seventeen. Years later my IQ was tested at 130.

My mother was a good person. She never smoked, rarely drank, found it impossible to lie and found it unnecessary to curse. I use to say that if the devil came to the door asking for me, she would have to point me out. She just couldn't lie. Keeping that in mind I believe these stories about my father. He was gone most of the time. "Looking for work mostly," he'd say. He once left my mother and I, infant at the time, in a truck box with nothing but a case of canned milk. He was gone for weeks.

She eventually made her way to Lincoln City, Oregon and went to work at the Dorchester House when it was a restaurant. They had a horseshoe-shaped lunch counter/coffee shop in one area and a large dining room overlooking a huge well-maintained flower garden. She had a room upstairs and had herself or various co-workers look in on me when she was on shift.

The owner of the Dorchester at that time was a man by the name of Jeroff. He must have been a very patient, giving man. Nine days after I turned two-years old, my sister was born. Mom said it was one of her weaker moments during a visit by my father that my sister, Carol, was conceived. By the time she was born, Mr. Jeroff had moved mom and me into a cottage behind the Dorchester. The first moments of my life that I remember were in that cottage when mom brought my sister home.

I remember Mr. Jeroff later in life when I became his assistant gardener at the age of about 12 or 13. In one incident, the gas mower broke and I had to mow the huge lawn behind the Dorchester House with a push mower. For several weeks, on Tuesdays and Fridays, I would go back and forth pushing that reel mower without much of a break.

We mowed it twice a week and I began to look forward to it when diners in the restaurant would send tips down to me, probably feeling sorry for me. I believe the admiration of the diners and the tips (of course) contributed to my work ethic then and later in life. Using an internet program, I measured the lawn at just under a half acre.

My mother said several times, people had wanted to adopt my sister and me. I suppose they saw a single mother with two kids struggling to get by. She was always proud of the fact that she turned them down.

While working at the Dorchester, mom met my first stepfather. He was a heavy smoker, drank too much at times, cussed like a sailor and was a born liar when it came to his infidelities with other women. I guess in women's eyes that he was incredibly handsome. He was in Lincoln City for a construction job as he was a construction equipment operator and ate at the Dorchester coffee shop.

It soon became apparent that our new stepfather did not accept my sister and I for what we were. We inherited our mother's gentle caring nature and were extremely sensitive. From when he and my mother were married in October of 1947 until his accidental death in March of 1960, he only showed kindness to me on one occasion and he was drunk at the time. I don't know if it was something in his upbringing or not but he just could not give us the fatherly attention my sister and I, as stepchildren, needed.

On the contrary, his verbal abuse was rampant. I don't remember being struck with his hand or fist vary often, it did happen, but his favorite form of discipline was a rather hard kick. They were enough to lift me off the floor and he hurt my sister badly on several occasions. Discipline of unruly kids could be understood but my sister and I were always on good behavior, especially when my stepfather was near. We had to be quiet and move fast when told to do so. We did not push or challenge him at all, his methods where too strong. He just had a mean temper. The abuse was felt more in that my sister and I were so sensitive.

There were some things that I admired about my stepfather. He was a Seabee trained equipment operator and took part in the battle of the Pacific during World War II. He worked for a sand and gravel company in Lincoln City and slowly bought his own equipment. He eventually went into business for himself and was very good at what he did. I use to brag about the various jobs he did around Lincoln County where we lived. He did instill in me a strong work ethic, as I worked for him on many jobs. I worked as hard as I could so as not to invoke his wrath.

My mother and her new husband had another child, a girl, and my stepfather loved her very much. He showed all his affection on her. I never held it against her that he favored her and enjoyed being raised with her as my sister. Years later when I had several children of my own, I found myself falling into the same abuse-sharing pattern. Two of my sons were from my wife's previous marriage. It finally came to me that I was just like him and I put a stop to it. I eventually spoke to my boys about it and felt that I could not apologize enough to them. I spent a lot of time in therapy and discovered just how much damage child abuse did to me and others around me.

Little did I know how much my stepfather's verbal and physical abuse would affect me. It wasn't until those therapy sessions when I was 50-years-old that I discovered what he had done. Some of those effects I will keep to myself and will follow me to the grave. I am in my seventh decade of life and I can identify residual effects of the abuse I suffered during those formidable twelve years. From an early age I had an undying need to please my stepfather. He never gave even so much as a "Good job!" or even a simple "Thank you."

I worked for him in his excavation company and worked hard. As my life progressed, the greatest affect was on my work ethic. I always had to give 110 percent. If you wanted more I gave it plus ten percent more. Outside of the military, my longest work day was twenty-five hours.

Sometimes it would spiral out of control. One of my last jobs involved voluntary sixteen hour days, seven days a week.

Finally, I collapsed on the worksite. The job ended soon after that; I would have probably worked myself to death.

Gaining a strong work ethic at such an early age led me to the realization that if I wanted money, I had to work for it. I learned that the more I worked, the more I earned. I soon earned the confidence of the neighborhood and did all sorts of odd jobs to earn money. The usual stuff was mowing lawns, clearing brush or weeding flower and shrub beds.

In the 50's those that could not afford septic systems would use fifty-five gallon drums buried in the ground with a concert tile line running several feet for the run off. I became very good at digging new systems for the neighborhood and our own house. There were no controls in those days so we had a drum in the ground for two adults and three children. I don't remember how long each drum would last but it seemed I was always doing one for someone.

One of the ladies in the area always seemed to have small jobs for me and I liked the pay. Mostly weeding or mowing. I cannot remember if she was married or not or I just plain forgot if she had a husband. Either way, it soon became apparent that her interest in me was not only my ability to pull weeds. I must have been fourteen or so. She began telling me I need to take a break and would invite me in for a soda or something. She always seemed to be getting ready for work and liked to expose a little skin. She would not be classed as an attractive woman at all to most; short, a little chubby maybe. I would guess her age at about forty or forty-five, but much older than my mother.

Being shy though, I would not even think of anything sexual with her except in my fantasies. A first move was out of the question and I was scared to death when she started touching me. To be blunt, it didn't bother me at all and I was a willing partner. She knew she had me hooked from the first.

I was a virgin of course and at the age of fourteen my hormones were raging. How many fourteen-year-old boys do we know that would have said, "Hey, this is wrong and I don't want any part of it?" Not many, I would guess. As life progressed, a good share of my problems with sex was the lack of ability to say no to anything sexual.

We did not have intercourse. She just wanted to play with my penis and feel my chest and ass and she kept one of her hands between her legs most of the time. She let me touch her breasts sometimes and they were huge. I think that started me on that road of loving big breasts with large nipples. Doesn't every man?

I was with her probably half a dozen times or so. As this was my first sexual interaction with an adult woman, I felt extremely lucky. Of course it was the hottest thing that ever happened to me up to that time. When I was not with her, she and other women were all I could think about. I mean, I had plenty of fantasies. Now that I know what all those women were hiding under their clothes, I didn't have to use half-dressed pictures in the magazines and catalogs, for there were none around the house anyway. Porn was hard to get in the fifties for a fourteen-year-old.

I think now, later in my life, that she had a guilt trip and just stopped having me over. At the time, I was over-whelmed with a sense of loss and abandonment. She would wave when we saw each other but that was it. My shyness prevented me from asking for anything other than if her yard needed work. On the couple of occasions that I approached her for work, she smiled and told me she needed the exercise and was doing the work herself.

The Sex Club

The county that I grew up in had a well hidden sexual underground, let's call it a club. Much later in life I learned of several people I know in the community that was participants and members. I learned of at least two of my schoolmates that were drawn in, willingly or unwillingly I don't know. They were very withdrawn most of the time, like me I think. I will not name names.

Unbeknownst to me, my stepfather was a member. I now believe that because of my step fathers activities and association with this club that it was assumed that I was fair game.

I spent a lot of my time with him in his work because it just made economic sense to use me as a worker for free rather than hire someone for wages. I learned at a young age to work like a man even if it hurt. To physically keep up with my stepfather, as I grew older, I became very strong. Not wanting to stand out, I kept my strength well hidden from my school mates. As my stepfather did not want my mother to know what he was up to, he kept me out of the loop.

Abusing teenagers seemed to be one of the club's activities, but not on a large scale. Over the years I recall the two other boys involved and I knew of only one girl so I cannot say that abusing teenagers was widespread.

After my stepfather's death, there were a few attempts to draw me in on the phone. About three times or so I would get an anonymous phone call and be propositioned for gay sex. That scared me every time. A male voice would make small talk like I was supposed to know who he was and then he would tell me what he would like to do to me. It did not sound very comfortable.

I would hang up and get my stepfather's shotgun out of the closet in case they were watching my house. We didn't have caller ID in those days and I didn't know who was calling. Curiosity didn't enter my mind. At that young age, I didn't know males did those things to each other.

My stepfather was known to be sexually involved with several women and more than two of my mother's "best friends." He was a handsome devil and the ladies loved him. My mother found out about her friends activities with her husband after he was killed. In her grief state we talked about it a lot. I was her sounding board I think, for I believe she could not talk to others about it. Perhaps she felt a lot of shame and a little blame.

She admitted that she did not like sex much anyway and that may have drove her husband stray. I think it would have happen anyway. She was a little more than angry at her friends but it was her nature not to hate.

I recall when working with him on one job, we drove farther into the mountains that I never knew existed. He had to correct a drainage job with his power shovel or excavator as they are known today. He had moved his machine to the far end of the farm days earlier when I was not with him but when he wanted to move it back, he brought me with him to drive his pickup back.

He said to wait at the farm house as it would take over an hour to crawl back at the speed of his machine. He introduced me to the attractive lady at the house and told her to leave me alone, grinning with some secret message passing between them.

I parked my dad's truck in the driveway and getting in on the passenger side, figured I would have a long wait. I wanted to explore some of the farm buildings there but not knowing the lady I thought it best to just sit and wait. The lady came out of the house and directly up to the truck. She stood on the running boards on my side and leaned over to talk to me.

She had on one of those sun dresses with the loose top and I'm sure now, her intention was to give me a full view of what I then thought was the best part of a woman's body. At that time I was sure it was an accident and would only let my eyes wonder when she looked away. She looked away a lot and now that I reflect upon it, I am sure that looking away was part of her game.

She must have led a boring life being so far back in the woods. Her husband worked in town and she kept talking about a variety of subjects. At the age of fifteen, obviously, I was not too versed at conversing with attractive, loosely dressed, thirty-something-year-old women. Today, I think we call them cougars.

She eventually told me I did not have to wait in the truck and invited me in for the inevitable soda, milk, or something. I was reluctant to get out of the truck as I had an erection by now and did not want anyone to ever see that. Not being sexually aggressive due to my shyness and not knowing I was being played, I did decide to give into her invitation because she smelled so nice.

When we got inside, she sat me down at the dining table but facing the kitchen. She got something out of the refrigerator, sat it on the table and squatted in front of me. My God, she wasn't wearing any panties! Shyness be dammed! All I could do was stare, all the while hoping she would not move and did not mind me looking. That was my first view of a live, warm, and real pussy; up until that moment, all other views were in magazines, stashed in my bedroom. She put her hand on the inner part of my thigh and asked, "Do you have a girlfriend?"

"Y-yes, but we don't do anything," I stammered.

"Why not?" she asked. But before I could answer, she said, "Let me show you what she should be doing that's safe."

She stood up, guiding me up with one of my hands and using her other hand, she started unbuckling my jeans. My hard on was raging by now and I hoped I was about to lose my virginity. Whatever was about to happen, again, I sure was not about to say no. She expertly dropped my pants, and on her knees, she cupped my testicles and started giving me oral sex. It didn't take long as it was my first and I found out just how much she liked the stuff that came out of my penis.

"How was that?" she purred.

I don't recall what I said but you can bet it probably couldn't be understood. I do remember being pleased but also embarrassed and a little scared too. I also remembered being worried about being caught with a mess but she cleaned me up real proper and began to make small talk, saying, "Your dad will be back soon."

Just as she assured, my stepfather returned and parked the machine out of the way. It dawned on me that he had to bring his dump truck and equipment trailer back to haul it away sometime later in the week. I hoped he would need me to help but I knew, probably not. My duties at my summer job kept me busy and I only worked with my stepfather on split shifts or days off.

I wanted to see the pretty lady again, but even if given the wonderful opportunity, I am sure I would not know how to act or what to do. I probably would have been embarrassed to look in her direction. Even then, I was having a difficult time keeping an eye on her, flashbacking to an hour earlier on the fact that she had my penis in her mouth.

I went out to the pickup to wait when my stepfather went in to get paid. When he came out to the truck, I noticed immediately he was visibility upset. With the abuse he passed out to my sister and I, we could tell when he was mad. His face would get a steely, hard look. At the time, I assumed that maybe it was payment for the job or something. We never talked much, if at all.

A day or two later I asked if he needed help moving the shovel. His abrupt no told me it was something else. Thinking back, she may have assumed I could be a target for their club activities. Having straightened her out, now he had to pretend he knew nothing about it. Putting me in his place, I would consider that a close-call. Together, we never went back and I never saw the lady again—well maybe just in a thousand fantasies. I had thoughts of someday having a car and driving out there to see her but, what if her husband was there? How would I explain myself? Lost, maybe?

I always thought of myself as being oversexed. My interest in sex started at a very early age. Remembering how sensitive

I have been my entire life and especially those early years, about the age of six I was caught messing around and was very traumatized by the whole thing. I think this made me extremely shy, sexually, and kept me afraid of being caught reacting to any sexual notions.

When I became mature enough to decipher my feelings, I realized that I was just extremely reckless. The older I became, the more I realized how deeply ingrained this recklessness was. I did not discuss my experiences with these ladies with my buddies as most teenagers would have. I just could not stand the thought of talking about my erection with anyone, let alone someone of my age. As teens, we would joke about sex but any participation in sex talk about me was a taboo subject as far as I was concerned.

Another one of my escapes was to wander the woods on the Oregon coast. I had many amazing adventures. I would hunt, fish and trap or just explore. When I was about fifteen, I partnered with a neighbor friend and we caught about 200 beaver. A little older, he taught me how to set traps, skin and prepare the catch for sale and where to go to get beaver. In turn I would help him pack out the catch and help with the skinning. I soon got my own traps and started my own trap line around a lake near my home. I did fairly well with mink, muskrat and small animals.

On one of those trips to the woods, I hit my knee on a very sharp axe and cut the main tendon at the knee cap. I was fourteen and I remember seeing the edge of the bone through the hole in my knee and my leg went limp. I guessed it wouldn't work without that tendon. I had a friend with me and he got a little pale when he saw the bone. I put a splint on my leg and managed to make it to the edge of the woods.

My friend ran ahead and got my mother to bring the car to pick me up. The local doctor by the name of Peabody deadened my knee and tried to find the tendon with his finger for what seemed to be hours. He finally realized I needed to go to Portland and arranged it. My mother took me in her car and I spent eight months in recovery after the hospital.

I would also sneak out of my second story bedroom at night and just walk the beach. Sometimes but not always, I would leave the house without the proper coat or clothing for the beach winds. This meant the only way to keep warm on the way home was to keep moving and get the walk over. It was on one of those beach walks early in the morning that I discovered that I had something special.

I spotted a huge log far up the beach in the dryer sand area. I usually avoided that area because it was hard walking. The log was about five feet in diameter and twenty-five feet long. I saw a three foot gap in the top of the log and was immediately drawn to that gap. All of this on a very dark night in a light mist. When I got to the hole in the log I was surprised to see it was full of water with sand in the bottom and an Asian fishing float. The hole was formed by fire.

What was unusual about this is the power of attraction I felt to check out that gap in the log and the nature of my find. Additionally, I knew how the hole in the log was formed but unsure how the sand and the glass float got into a floating object and stayed there, while the log would roll around beaching itself. This special-something did not manifest itself with enough regularity for me to put a finger on it and try to recognize or control it. Rather it would just happen and I would just have enough time to say, "There it is again."

The one thing that I believe got me through my childhood years with some sense of sanity was Jessie Marian Sharp. We went to separate schools for the first five years but started the sixth grade in 1955 together. We were twelve-years-old. She seemed to be very shy and she was so cute. It was puppy love at first sight for me.

We were inseparable in school and got together whenever we could, sometimes with our parents providing a ride to a movie or school event. I can remember her and I going shopping in the big city with my mother in the 1956 Chevrolet my parents owned at the time. Mom would go shop and Jessie and I would write notes back and forth in the back seat. We were both that shy. It took me two years to work up the courage to kiss her. Yes, two years!

In around 1958 we broke up for a year or so. Probably due to my immaturity, I still haven't grown up to this day. During that year I went steady with another girl in our class who was to become my second wife later in life. After a few months, the steady did not work out and some of our high school friends invited Jessie and I to a hay ride to sort of get us back together. It worked and we were a pair until 1961. Most of us remember how intense that first love is. Even though it is classified as puppy love, it is something we never forget. Jessie was on my mind for the rest of my life.

I had one incident in my youth that was years in the making. One of my buddies and I, whom I will not name as he had a girlfriend, were out cruising in the middle of the night. It was during that period I had broken up with Jessie. Another school mate stopped us and told us he had arranged a meeting with three Mennonite girls on holiday at a motel near the beach. They were going to sneak out past their chaperons after midnight and we were to pick them up. Hey, we were fifteen and had to move on this one. Naturally we were highly excited.

"What the hell was a Mennonite anyway?" I asked.

My buddies said it was some religious sect from the Valley. We picked them up, two in the front and four in the back of my friend's car. We drove out to Sand Point and two left for the bushes, leaving me and another girl in the back seat. Those in front were down low so we had some privacy but I was still nervous and shy about everything. No worry, the girl with me wanted to start some heavy necking and right now.

We got as prone as you could in the cars of the 50's and she had one of my legs in her crotch. I could feel her pelvic bone and what it had with it hot on my leg. I naturally had a huge erection and she did not touch it with her hands but she knew it was there and brushed up against it as much as she could. I don't know if anyone scored or not, I don't remember. I didn't and would not with all those people around anyway.

What made the story unusual is I gave the girl my phone number and throughout the years, maybe four or five times, she would call me. I had gotten back with Jessie, or married my first wife, or married my second wife or for whatever reason, a relationship was just not to be. The last time she called I was at my mother's house with my second wife and four kids. It had to be over ten years after we had met at Sand Point. I will never know how she got my mother's Salem, Oregon phone number. I will never know why a woman would put so much stock into a ten-year make out session.

When I turned sixteen it was finally time to get my driver's license. I had a learner's permit so my friend Harry, who had his license, drove me home from school to get my parent's car to take the test. My stepfather had bought me a 1950 Plymouth but it would not be the best car to take the test in, so mom's new 1959 Chevrolet would have to do. When I passed the test, we drove home first and then headed back to school. I was in my Plymouth and Harry was in front of me. School got out before we could make it back. One of the busses had stopped to let passengers off and I was so intent on trying to see if it was Jessie's bus that I forgot to stop and totaled both of our cars in a rear end collision.

3

IN THE ARMY

The spring of 1960 was when I was forced to grow up and move on from childhood. My stepfather, who raised me and had a huge negative influence on my life, was killed in an unusual accident involving his construction equipment. Regardless of his evil temperament, I always admired what my stepfather had accomplished and his participation in the war. Every time he would beat, kick or verbally abuse me, I just could not get past the strength of the abuse.

"Was I that bad? Did he hate me that much?"

I found myself wishing him dead and wondered what it would be like if he was killed. After he died, I felt horrible. I felt that I was partly responsible for his death. Many years later, my sister and I were discussing how his death affected us and we discovered she had the same feelings of joy and then guilt. She had also wished him dead.

I cannot believe how fast life took off after that. He left behind my mother, of course, my sister from mom's first marriage and my sister who was my stepfather's only child. So mom was about 33, a widow, and had three kids to raise on her own. That's not unusual in today's world but being "not unusual" does not make it easy.

I was in my third year of high school and found out that I would not be able to graduate with my class. I was smart and had a high IQ but in my efforts to get away from my stepfather's verbal and physical abuse, I spent too much time in the woods hunting or trapping critters or fishing any body of water from streams to the ocean. I became very good at becoming a modern day "mountain man" for lack of a better name for my activities.

School work was on the bottom of my list of things needed to survive in this world. My mother and I were very close but not close enough for her to get me to improve my grades. She was also too busy working jobs outside the home so we could maintain the lifestyle brought on by the end of World War II. Now that the family breadwinner was gone, my mother knew she was on her own. With the help of people that my stepfather worked with and for, she sold off his equipment and got by very well once I decided to leave home.

Since I was only 17-years-old, a parent had to sign authorization for me to get into the service. On or near my birthday in August, my mother accompanied me to the recruiting station in Portland, Oregon. She signed the necessary papers and went shopping and visiting my aunt, who lived in Portland, while I took the entrance exams and a physical.

The tests are used to determine what recruits' aptitudes, abilities and interests are, and were used to place the man into a career field. All but one of my tests scored in the highest level. As I said, I was smart but did not want to use my brain. High school, in my mind, was a waste of time.

My stepfather's influence on me, and my sister for that matter, was devastating. Had I been encouraged to develop I could have been and done anything I wished. The tests they used then must have been created by a simpleton. A few years later, I was in a position to administer those same tests. I could max out any one of almost all of the tests.

My weakness was verbal expression. In high school I failed all of my English, vocabulary, writing or verbal expression classes. As I did not have a high school diploma, I was allowed to enter the service but it was noted in my records that I needed to take the GED High School Equivalence Test.

The recruiter, a senior Non-commissioned Officer, or better known as an NCO (which from henceforth will be used often), told me I could choose almost any career field I wanted because my scores were so high. I always admired airplanes so I told him I wanted to be an aircraft mechanic. I signed a paper in which the US Army guaranteed training as a basic aircraft mechanic.

The way it worked was the government would sign up a group of recruits like me and have them report in when they had a sizable group. I was told to come back on August nineteenth and I would be sworn in and be on my way to being a soldier.

I went on one more fishing trip to central Oregon with a friend. I really enjoyed the trip. The weather was perfect and I caught a lot of fish. We camped in an area with many lakes that were well stocked with hatchery and natural trout.

Fast forward twenty-seven years for just a moment. The love of my life, Jessie, and I were making a trip through that same area and camped at the same site. Nothing had changed. It seemed as not one grain of dust had changed. Even the fire pit was in the same place. I'm sure the trees had grown but it still looked the same to me. It was one of those Déjà vu moments.

On the August nineteenth, I and the others met a bus at the recruiting office and we were transported to the Portland, Oregon airport. The plane they put us on was a two engine propeller driven aircraft. It was not the best choice for a person's first flight and I was a little apprehensive. Every movie a person would see with an airplane in it would crash the plane. Back then, I was scared but my vocabulary has advanced so now I can say I was "apprehensive." We were flown to an airport somewhere near, but not part of, Fort Ord, California, to start our basic training.

It wasn't long before men were yelling at me. There was no pleasing them.

"Too slow!"

"Too fast!"

"Too high!"

"Not loud enough!"

"Too dull!"

"Too shiny!"

"It's dirty...," and all kinds of adjectives I never heard before. I had enough of that from my stepfather. I was just past my 17th birthday and highly impressionable. It wasn't long before I wanted out. True to my nature though, I stuck to it and did everything they said to do. I found out that to stay out of the way was to get out front of everyone where no one could catch me anyway. Give it all and then some and they ignored me while they yelled at those in the back.

The basic training program they used at that time did a good job of leveling men out. The rifle range was a good example. A good percentage of the men in our company had never shot a gun; many had never even held one. There were men from all over the country and those from the big cities were the ones with no shooting experience, they knew nothing about guns. On the other hand there were many like I who had been hunting and shooting a good share of their lives and knew it all and assumed they did not need any help. Those that knew nothing had no choice but to listen to the instruction and follow directions to the tee. They did well.

We shot targets as far away as 500 yards. They were giant bull's eyes the size of at least four foot square or human sized silhouettes from the waist up that would pop up for a few seconds to offer target opportunity. It was not easy to teach a novice how to become an expert shooter at those distances when they had no experience. Again, those that listened did well and most were awarded the expert badge when it was all over.

On the other hand, we had that bunch of know-it-all's that didn't need help shooting targets, especially targets that weren't moving. Many of the latter embarrassed themselves by scoring below expert. They assumed their methods were better and failed to see the benefit of a military marksman program. You should know already where I came out. I was always afraid not to follow directions and questioned nothing and shot expert, of course.

The process of leveling men out worked well when it came to body weight also. Those that entered basic too fat, lost weight, and those that were too skinny, gained. The program would shove calories in and try to run you to death, at least I thought so. I gained some muscle by eating everything I could and doing more than asked in the physical training program.

The company I was assigned to lost a cook to a transfer. So, near the end of my training cycle, maybe three weeks, they pulled me out of training. I was told to relax, ignore the things going on around me, keep my mouth shut, and help out in the kitchen.

It wasn't too bad. I hated all the discipline and regimentation going on around me. When I got to my assigned unit months later, I discovered they put me through a lot of training on paper. I remember there were some things I just had to do and they would make me participate in training those days.

Near the end of basic training when things were relaxing, families were invited to our graduation. My mother received flowers for traveling the farthest to attend the ceremony, about 700 miles. I was chosen to give a demonstration on tearing the M-1 rifle down and reassembling it while wearing a blindfold.

My mother's brother was stationed at Fort Ord and I was allowed to go off base with my mother to visit him and his family. My uncle was an engineer and operated earth moving equipment. He lived off base in an area city called Seaside. We also did a tour of the area to see places we had heard about but have not seen, such as Carmel by the Sea. Going through basic training was the longest I had ever been away from home and I was absorbing the new life experiences like a sponge.

After finishing basic, I was given two weeks leave. That's US Army talk for vacation. I went to my home town, of course, to show off my uniform and see my girlfriend, Jessie. I began to realize that I was on my own and was no longer a part of the household I grew up in. I had a career and no more wasting time in school. I would have walked through fire to get out of the regimentation of school work. Little did I realize that school would be a cake walk in view of what was coming.

I reported in to the replacement company on Fort Lewis, Washington in late October, 1960. Men and women just out of basic training stand out like new born babies in their exuberance and zeal, following every order like they're about to be shot if they don't. After observing how things are out of basic, they relaxed a little and fit in rather than react with obvious demeanor of a newbie. The principle reason for wanting to fit in may be because others around them love to pick on them for laughs.

I soon learned my first lesson in guarantees from the Army. I wanted to be an aircraft mechanic and they guaranteed me training. I suppose to soften the blow of their half-assed attempt at schooling in the field, they assigned me to Fort Lewis. That was the closest base to my home town that I could be assigned to. I liked that but what I didn't like was the training. I was assigned to the 4th Aviation Company, 4th Infantry Division to receive OJT, called on-the-job training, as a basic aircraft mechanic. No formal schooling, but just let someone teach me how to work on their aircraft. A basic mechanic is not much, usually keep the aircraft clean and check the oil.

As my time in the service progressed, I learned many men were entered into their career field this way. They would qualify for the basic knowledge and then apply for advanced schooling later and actually did better as they had some experience by the time they got to schooling. It worked well.

As for my OJT, when I got to the unit, the administration NCO looked at my record and the high aptitude scores and asked me if I wanted to work in his office. As it was raining outside and men were working at the inclement airfield, I told him I would give it a try. Besides, I always had to try and please any one in front of me first. Thus, began a long career in administration. High aptitude scores took me many desirable places in the service.

I stayed with the 4th Aviation Company for about twenty-two months. During that time, I was a klutz; a very good one too. It wasn't intentional; I just fell all over myself trying to please everyone. I couldn't keep my uniforms neat and clean. My area always seemed to have a little dust. My bed was never tight enough. I didn't like physical training, I hated inspections, I was afraid of authority.

On one occasion, the company was scheduled for a very important inspection. They loaded up a large truck with stuff they did not want to get caught with, like excess equipment and such. They told me to get in the truck and drive around post all day and not show up until about 4pm. They did not want me around either. My uniform always looked shabby and I just could not wear it right. In truth, I was the company sad sack. I always tried my best but it just did not work for me. I was not rebellious at all, I was just inept.

It was common practice to rotate field rations left over from the wars by feeding them in the mess hall once a month. They would open all the cans of the various kinds of content and combine them in pots and give the men a choice of what they wanted. They would put all the candy packs in pots and pass them out too. These rations contained cigarettes in packs of five or six or full packs of twenty.

When I came to the server behind the cigarettes in the chow line, he would offer them and when I refused as I did not smoke, he would ask me to take them and pass them out to my buddies. The cigarettes were old, years old and very distasteful so no one wanted them.

I was still an impressionable seventeen-year-old and everyone said smoking was alright. So I eventually got around to trying a pack of Pall Malls that I bought at the Post Exchange. It sure tasted good and I was hooked. Cigarettes and smoking was considered safe, so much so that it was scheduled into daily activities. A military unit operated with a daily training schedule and smoke breaks were written into that document when in a classroom environment.

A call came down from higher headquarters for the 4th Aviation Company to detail a clerk to the Fort Lewis School Command. Naturally, they decided to send me. I was a good worker but a sloppy soldier. The School Command was in another part of the post and I was to be the company clerk. Duty was laid back and I spent several months there. I excelled because there was no pressure of physical training, inspection and the duty week was only five days, unlike at the 4th Aviation Company where the duty week included Saturday mornings. I finally decided I liked the Army a little.

Good things have to come to an end. We had an incident called the Cuban Missile Crisis. All of the people detailed around the post were sent back to their units and I was not allowed to go back when the crisis was over.

One of the highlights of my early time in the US Army was meeting and serving with many WW II and Korean War Veterans. They had been in combat and were good at passing on what they had learned to stay out of trouble. When we went to the field for training, they were very serious about their training. Many of them bore the scars of war, not just physical but mental as well. Some were deeply affected and they were just doing their time to get their retirement. They were of some use and it was good that the government let them stay in the service.

I remember one veteran of the Bataan Death March. He had white blotches of hair all over his head and was of very calm demeanor. It wasn't until years later that I learned what he had been through. I know he did not want to talk of his experience but I wish I could have found some way to thank him. Many of these veterans had a manner of shaking their head or hands in a nervous tic.

I am sure they are all dead now and that makes me sad that I did not attempt to learn more from them. They mostly did not want to talk of their experiences but I would have liked to have met them all as the heroes they were.

If ever needed, I would hope that the young people of to-day would come through as the young men and women did during the period of 1941-1945 that we call World War II. In my grateful opinion, this world would be a better place if they took some of the so-called reality trash off of television and make the history of World War II a required course in high school.

The Black Experience

I experienced my first run in with racial discrimination during this time period. Up until my enlistment into the service, I had not interacted with Black Americans. I took to them right away and enjoyed being around them. I made friends with a man my age, last named Alsup. We were always hanging around and pulling jokes on each other like the teens that we were.

I was going to my home in Lincoln City on some weekends when I could afford it, so I invited Alsup to go with me and meet my family. I told him we would go out with my sister for a Coke or something. Some rednecks from the southern states over heard me talking to Alsup and later cornered me alone to inform me that Whites and Blacks did not mix that way. I felt they were threatening me and I made excuses to Alsup. Thinking back, if I had a spine I would have stood up to them and probably got my ass beat, but that was not in my make-up at that time.

I became friends with many Black Americans over the years and have a genuine love for that race of men and women. I admire their struggle to overcome their status in our early history. Part of that struggle was the fact that during WW II, they were mostly put into service jobs and were treated as if they were incompetent to perform on the front lines of combat.

President Truman ordered integration of the military and with struggle, it worked. Society could have gotten a head start accepting our Black Americans if technology would have allowed us to make the movie of the *Tuskegee Airman* available. That movie is on my list of favorites that non-regrettably I watch over and over again.

Not being demeaning or insulting, but I find it very ironic that if those who practice racism were to open their mind's eye, they would see that African-Americans' mental capabilities are just like Whites. Yes, like us, there are many genii among them.

I love studying history. One aspect of our American history that I am very fond of is African American. One figure of many in particular is George Washington Carver. In my humblest opinion, he was a true genius.

As my career in the military matured, I had many Black friends. I found no discrimination around me after those early incidents. I served with many that had been promoted up the chain of command and no complaints of being held back because of race. On the contrary, I can recall a few attempts by others at mild off color jokes and those around such activity were quick to point out that it was neither appropriate nor funny. There were usually no Black soldiers around when these incidents took place so they were not aware of it.

I was proud to be a part of the comradery in the military with Black and White together. We see in movies about Viet Nam and such where Black soldiers would gaggle together and as a living witness, they did. But Whites did the same thing.

I am sure there was discrimination; however, given the mentality and cultural background of most Whites whom I served with, I knew better to believe that just because I did not see it did not mean that it was inexistent. In reverse, many Black Americans did not see the quick reaction by White soldiers to squelch jokes involving race, or any other form of favoritism.

I am sure discrimination was a huge problem to many. I can't speak for others, but I believe that racist attitudes—no matter how they were created in the individual—are like cursing; it shows a weakness of the mind and its capability to properly and respectfully express oneself. How do we get past that?

Losing Jessie

Around the time of Jessie's high school graduation, and running with the wrong group of guys, I broke it off and hurt her really bad. Jessie and I were together about six years over a seven year period from middle school, through high school, my entry into the Army, and we never had sex.

Instead of going to her high school graduation, I went to a gathering of men and girls in Yakima that had been arranged by some of my friends during our training there. I called Jessie from Yakima just before her high school graduation ceremony and told her I was not going to make it there. I'm sure it was very hurtful for her, as she heard what was going on in the background. That is just one example of many of the stupid decisions I have made over my life. It may have been one of those birds in the hand things.

I assumed I had a chance at my first sex in Yakima. The pedestal I had placed Jessie on was too high for me to instigate a sexual relationship with her. We did the heavy petting thing and we stopped each other on numerous occasions from going that final step to all the way. I don't know what planet my decision process was on, but I was still a teenage male hunting his first sex.

All of us men remember this time of our life and women cannot experience the same feelings. Of course we men cannot relate to the female equivalent feelings. It is just one of life's trials that we have to get through. I believe that the male is rather reckless in this stage.

I developed a relationship with a girl my age in Yakima. Her name was Donnie. I began going to Yakima instead of my hometown. We got into some heavy petting for a while and I worked up the courage to touch her female attributes. She let me know it was ok so I figured maybe I would finally lose my virginity.

Donnie had very pale skin and blond hair. She was not what most would call an attractive girl but I did not care what she looked like as long as her sex organs didn't swing when she walked. Finally, Donnie's mother had to go out of town for the weekend so Donnie had her best friend stay with us as a chaperone. They both agreed that Donnie and I were going to have sex that weekend and her friend would just stay out of the room. Donnie's friend was a beautiful woman and when all things were over, I wished that I could have gotten past my shyness and muster the courage to ask her out.

That first evening alone, Donnie shyly stripped naked and got into the bed. Then I did the same, trying to hide my enormous erection. We kissed a little and I got on top of her and put the head of my penis on the opening of her vagina. Any experienced lover would have known of all the things to do to a woman at that point. Getting her more ready would have been a wise idea. She was just so easy and cooperative, ready for sex. I think she saw the size of my penis and may have had misgivings about having that huge chunk of meat shoved into her body. I gave a little push thinking, finally. She gave out a muffled scream and pushed me back. She said she couldn't do it.

Ever the gentleman, I nonchalantly said, "That's okay." Telling Donnie I had to pee, I went to the bathroom to masturbate of course, justified after coming closer than I had ever come before to losing my virginity. We said our goodbyes the next day and I never went back.

I felt a great sense of loss as I had given up my long relationship with Jessie in favor of chasing the possibility of sex. Now, that was gone also. Had I stayed with Jessie I would have probably strayed and after a child or two, the marriage would have ended. That seems to be the common scenario in today's times. Additionally, I was preloaded later in life with an insatiable need for sex with many women.

Within months of my breakup with Jessie and the Yakima incident, one of the high school bad girls invited me into her life. She was a few months younger than me and I was innocent of her other carnal activities. Unbeknownst to me, she was a sexual predator. What a wild ride. My first sex was with her and she became my first wife.

She was seventeen and I was eighteen when we got married in Washington State. My mother knew of my new wife's background and refused to sign for me to get married under the age of twenty-one. However, there was a law in Washington State regarding military members that allowed for an adult to sign for a minor if the legal guardian of the minor was out of state. I don't know how it worked but it did.

As life progressed, and thinking back, I came to realize that sex with my first wife could have been amazing if I knew what I was doing. In my shyness and inexperience I was terrible at sex. Of all the embarrassing things I must write to tell my story, the one I really wish to avoid is the fact that it took me at least a year to open my eyes during sex. How innocent is that? I did my best, as in all endeavors, to please to the best of my ability but I would climax much too soon. That is not the way to satisfy a woman sexually. It took me even more years to get that right.

I had dreams of a different direction in the Army so in the summer of 1962 I reenlisted for a career in computer repair. Schooling this time was guaranteed and was to take place at Fort Monmouth, New Jersey. My mother and I repaired our relationship and we drove to Provo, Utah to visit with my grandmother, which proved to be the last time I ever saw Grandma Jensen. I finished the trip to New Jersey by bus. There I was, in school again. Binary and octal math, which computers use for language, threw me for a loop.

My son Greg was born while I was station at Fort Monmouth. I was not present for his birth so in December of that year I decided to attempt a trip to Oregon. I bought a 1953 Mercury convertible for $50 from a friend. He received orders for Viet Nam and the car needed a transmission, thus, justifying the cheap price for the car. I made it as far as Twin Falls, Idaho. I had four riders to help pay for gas and dropped them off in Pennsylvania, Chicago, South Dakota, and Idaho. I did not sleep the entire trip as I had no insurance and did not trust anyone driving my car.

I hit a pavement break near Twin Falls and the car began to shake. I slowly drove it into town and had to leave it for repairs. I caught a Greyhound bus to Portland, Oregon and after boarding the bus, I didn't even hear the engine start. I slept all the way. Up until that time, I had never been able to sleep in a moving vehicle.

Life treated my first wife very badly and I will not speak ill of her and do not blame her for the way she was. She had all the experience I didn't have and soon got bored with me. In her letters, she told me who trained her sexually and how young she was when it started. I think she was reaching out for help at that time but I probably did not know how to re-act or how to handle the situation. I do not have the right to accuse without proof so I won't pass what she told me on to others. Again, without proof, I can only say that according to the military medical system I was lucky I survived marriage with her.

While stationed at Fort Monmouth, I was treated for several kidney infections. My system was a mess. I cut myself shaving and it became a festering sore on my face. A mosquito bit me and the same thing happen on my arm. The doctor kept me on medicine for several weeks and it seemed to clear up. I failed out of that school so the powers that be offered me schooling in the telephone exchange field. It did not go well there either. Wanting to pacify me a little, they offered me a station of my choice. I told them I wanted to go to Alaska.

I arrived in Fairbanks and Fort Wainwright in April of 1963. Spring warmth was just starting. There was daytime thawing and nighttime freezing. The sun was bright and the snow remaining on the ground was even brighter. My first impression of Alaska was the birch trees. As I was growing up, birch trees were rarely seen and used for a landscaping tool. I, like many, have always liked the qualities of the birch tree and now they were everywhere.

Alaska had only been a state for four years. They didn't even use paper money much, opting for silver dollars instead. You could feel the relationship of Fairbanks and its early history during the gold rush, the frontier mentality was ever present. In June, myself and two of my other buddies that had also arrived in April, decided it was time to risk an adventure in the wilds of Alaska.

We drove north on the Steese Highway a few miles and stopped at a country store in a wide spot in the road called Fox. They had one of those gas pumps with a glass container on top that you pumped what you paid for into the container and let gravity put it in your tank. I went inside and being thirsty, I picked up a can of Coke. They charged me a dollar! In 1963, a dollar for a cola was really expensive.

Fast forward, thirty-five years later: My wife and I along with another couple drove our vehicles north from Wasilla, Alaska to camp on the Chatanika River, several miles up the Steese Highway. No trace of the country store could be found but near there was a modern quick stop grocery and gas station. We stopped to top off our tanks and being thirsty, I went inside to pick up a can of Coke. They charged me a dollar! Not bad, I hope the price holds for another thirty-five years.

My duties at Fort Wainwright were in the personal office. I worked in Building 1555. I was always a speed demon, not running the halls on my duties but close to it. The work ethic instilled in me was probably responsible for my pace.

That first summer I became friends with a lady named Beatty S. She was in her mid-30s. She had met a man when she was in her 20s and they were to get married but he was killed. She explained that it was very hard on her and she was finally over it after so many years. She had met another man and he was moving to Alaska and they were going to get married. Beatty was very religious and it was understood that she had never been with a man, for she was still a virgin.

She asked me to help her move to an apartment in Fairbanks before her future husband transferred his government job to Alaska. Always needing to please, I gladly helped her move and we became good friends. Beatty and her new husband enjoyed having me over to their apartment, knowing that I was bored to tears in the barracks. I would cook for them and they would let me drink a little bourbon or whatever wine was on hand. Eventually they met their neighbor, a really beautiful widow in her 60s. I do not remember her name.

Until this time, I had only had sex with one woman. As I said, I was not good at it at all. Because of my makeup, pursuing women was not my thing as I was too shy and too much afraid of rejection. I was still only nineteen and too innocent to tell when I was being pursued until it hit me on the head. Beatty's neighbor invited me over several times to hang a picture or to reach something off a shelf or whatever. I, of course, had the usual fantasies that a 19-year-old would have but could not connect with the fact that all I had to do was to stop and she would have been all over me, and I could have had my way with her, more like the other way around.

Beatty and her husband informed us at a dinner party that they were leaving town for a day or two.

The neighbor lady leaned over and whispered in my ear, "That's ok honey. Come on over while they are gone and I have something you can eat." She was grinning at me, and grinning back at her, I did not know what that meant.

Months later, I figured that out, but it was too late for me to act. Life's changes had moved past all the in-town activity. My soon-to-be ex-wife had shoved my face into her pussy once and not knowing what was expected of me I just nosed around a little and enjoyed the smell. I certainly did not know that it was called eating pussy. When you are young, you are too embarrassed to ask our buddies who are talking about sex. "What does that mean?" We just fake it that we know what they are talking about and figure it out later. What a moron I must have been.

The legal drinking age may be twenty-one in most of the country but on the military posts things were a little loose. Most of those in the enlisted men's and NCO clubs would not get too quick to check the ID of young-looking soldiers who had volunteered to fight for the country. If they got out of hand with activity or too loud for those around them, they would be asked to leave.

I would go to club to drink alcohol. I was under age. On one of those trips I met Sergeant Eddie Thompson and his wife Mary. They were having dinner at the NCO club. I had taken a night job with the club; I needed the extra money for my upcoming divorce. As with all customers, I affronted a friendly attitude ahead of most others. Eddie and Mary picked up on it and invited me to their home.

One of the missions of the Army in interior Alaska is to train for cold weather operations. That meant that soldiers would go to the field and perform in temperatures far below zero. They invited me over many times for dinner or just to spend time as I was single and lived in the barracks.

Mary would get a little tipsy sometimes at dinner and come on to me a little. I seem to remember her trying to take off her blouse on one occasion. Eddie didn't get too upset; he would just tell her to act her age and quit trying to scare Art. Eddie told me to come on over when he went to the field and keep Mary and the kids company. I didn't mind because it got me out of the barracks and I was able to watch TV.

One night, I was on the couch watching TV and Mary said she was going to go upstairs and get ready for bed. She came back down in a see-through nightgown and sat on my lap. Her intentions were very apparent. I was as usual, shy, scared, more like petrified, but horny as ever. Giving into youthful recklessness, I choose to go with the flow.

As the kids were all asleep I let her lead me upstairs. I would definitely not classify myself as a seducer because of my inexperience, extreme shyness, fear of being caught, extreme fear of rejection and just plain being inept at pursuing women for sex. I had only had sex with my first wife and it had been several months as we were going through a divorce. So I was ready and willing. Mary was to be the second woman I had sex with. She was about thirty-five and I was nineteen.

We did not have a second carnal meeting. She did "loan" me out to her best friend who lived across the three building court in her neighborhood. These courts were part of the military quarter's areas on base for longer serving service members and their dependents. The neighbor was just another lonely cougar whose husband was ignoring her. Military duties were tough on soldiers and their wives alike, especially when those duties involved serving through an Alaskan winter.

Mary's friend and I flirted, planned "sexcapades," did a little petting, but nothing came of it. She would get me drunk and she liked to play with my penis but would not let me go beyond that. As usual, being sexually aggressive was not in my deck of cards so I lost out on another opportunity. Perhaps Mary told her I was a little too fast to climax to get any satisfaction from, I don't know. I had an enormous penis and no stamina. Let's compare it to a large sex toy vibrator with no batteries.

When I think back to those days and what happened between Mary, Eddie and I, I believe Eddie knew what was happening and perhaps, I was not the first to keep his wife happy and get her past the cabin fever that was so prevalent during those long, dark, cold winters.

My first trip on the Alaskan-Canadian Highway, better known as the Alcan, was with Eddie in the winter of 1963-64. We did the trip in his 1957 Plymouth station wagon. He was insistent that I would save money over the $100 that was the cost for a round trip air fare. Eddie was a schemer and I should have suspected something when he stopped in Fort Greely, Alaska, for a case of oil. On the trip, until we broke down in Quesnel, British Columbia, we got just over fiftty miles to the quart of oil. We made the trip in the month of February which is one of the coldest months of the year.

Sometime in late 1963 after my transfer to Fort Wainwright, Alaska, my appendix burst. There was no prior sign of being sick. I was just fine and went to lunch about noon. An hour later, I got a pain in my stomach that would not go away. I went to the hospital (the one my son Gene was born in) and they operated on me just in time. The military doctors told me it was probably an unknown poison.

While I was convalescing, the woman who eventually would become my second wife wrote me a letter to reconnect. She was the girl I went steady with during the year Jessie and I broke up in high school. I brought her and her two sons to Alaska and in September 1964 at the Fairbanks City Hall, we got married. Our son, Gene was born ten months later.

During the first two years of our marriage, life was hard on us because like many others in the military, we did not get much pay. My spending habits were not very mature either. We couldn't afford much of a car to qualify for the winters in interior Alaska and affording insurance was impossible which meant we could not get post tags to get on and off base.

My wife soon learned to bundle the kids up for below zero weather and pull them on the sled if she had to go to the store on base. We would call a taxi if we had to go to the commissary and haul a month's supply of groceries on payday and hope it lasted.

We did purchase a couple of vehicles. We owned a 1956 Desoto for a while and a 1956 Studebaker pickup. We did manage to sneak on and off base without post tags. These tags were issued after the vehicle was inspected for safety and mechanical condition. Starting and keeping a vehicle running at temperatures far below zero took real work in those times. Many times I would have to walk to work from our quarters. It was about three miles. Luckily the military-issued clothing was designed to allow me to function in the cold.

Those years from April 1963 until October 1965 in Alaska were one of the most influential periods of my life. Upon reporting into the base for processing, my high aptitude scores stood out and I was chosen to work in the personal office. As they were responsible for all new arrivals, "personal," as it was called, had the pick of the crop and would break a few rules to hand pick only the best. Assignment to a personal office was considered a very prestigious position and in the 1960s meant that everyone on base was your friend.

The use of computers was in its early stages and all administrative work was mostly accomplished with a typewriter and a phone. Modernization meant we were updated to an electric typewriter. Our equipment allowance would only allow one of these intrusively, enormous machines. I became the fastest typist in the office and was given the job of typing special orders. Almost nothing could be accomplished in the administrative field without these formatted orders, produced on a wax like device and processed through a mimeograph machine.

I remember well, the men I served with; Mahala, Mahurin, Johnson, Harlow, Driskel, McLenden and General Lipscomb. Usually I don't remember names as well but I remember them and what they were like.

In October of 1965, we departed Alaska as I was assigned to the war effort in Viet Nam.

4

VIET NAM

After a leave in Tillamook, Oregon, to settle the family, I flew by military charter to Bangkok, Thailand. As the plane was coming into the Bangkok Airport I got my first look at a foreign country. I was just twenty-two years-old and my brain was absorbing the difference of our two cultures at first sight. At that time the average income in Thailand was around $200 a year.

I once read an article that compared the arrival and presence of Americans in Thailand to space ships arriving in the United States with technology far beyond ours. The ships would be loaded with thousands of men who were eight feet tall, handsome, made a million dollars a year, had an eighteen inch penis, and would overpay for sex all night long in the nearest whorehouse.

In 1965, the war in Viet Nam was starting to really get off the ground and culture shock was running both ways. I had heard that the sex trade in Thailand was the answer to my insatiable need for sex. Towns near the military bases had plenty of facilities for entertaining the GIs.

Sex was cheap. A trip to a room with a prostitute, called a "short time" was only two dollars. It lasted just as long as the man would take and the woman would return to the bar until the next one came along. A long time, or overnight, would cost five dollars and usually meant a trip to the woman's home or a cheap room in the many hotels that sprang up for that purpose.

These hotels were like a building full of closets with a hole in the floor at the end of the hall they called a bathroom. I went to the local village with others until I could learn the ropes. It was safe enough for the men plying the local clubs and the town's people knew enough to keep it that way.

My first sexual encounter in Thailand was with a woman at a local club. It was a higher end club with a band and singers imitating American music. The women were displayed behind a large glass window and a gentleman would select one from about twelve and pay to sit or dance with them. Thai men with higher incomes frequented this club also.

You could buy Thai whiskey or beer or bring your own bottle and buy mix and ice from the club. The hourly rate for the women was about two dollars. After a trip or two to the club, she told me she would take me home for five dollars. Of course I said yes.

Being my first sex with a woman in Thailand, I did not know what to expect but she was beautiful. I later found out that she had just started at the club and I was her first foreigner also. That made it special in view of the crude nature of the sex trade in Thailand. She had not yet been hardened to a crude state where most whores eventually end up.

What I remember most was the moment I climaxed in her, an image of the devil flashed in my brain. It was my first sexual encounter outside marriage. I did not feel guilty at the time or immediately afterwards. Additionally, I am an atheist and do not believe in the devil. In fact, thinking about it over the years, I find it amusing.

The most unusual thing of a sexual nature happened to me in Thailand; a friend and I were literally picked up by two middle-aged Thai women. They appeared to be about thirty-five years old. There actions were far outside the norm. They were very pretty and well taken care of, showing signs of being of the upper crust of Thai society. Their skin was fair; their feet were not the spread out pattern of the barefoot country women. They apparently had servants as shown by the way they carried themselves.

My friend and I were walking on the sidewalk; they came up to us, grabbed us by the arm, started speaking Thai like they knew us forever and led us into an off street hotel. It was apparent what they wanted but it was so out of place that we couldn't believe our luck.

The sex was very conservative as it must be in upper Thai society but I will take any sex any time I can get it. Neither of them would let us touch their privates but their nipples did show that they were aroused. They paid the bill and we parted ways with smiles and giggles all around.

They only thing I would use to explain their actions would be that it were a revenge thing against their husbands as males frequented whorehouses often. The conservative nature of their sex probably explained one of the many reasons their husbands strayed.

I did not enjoy having sex with women that did not enjoy the act with me. I would guess it came from my need to please. It is not hard to tell when a woman is faking it. No matter what noises she makes, her body will tell if she is getting anything out of the encounter.

I finally met and entered a short-term relationship with a woman called Lik. She had two children and a place to live. It was safer to have only one sex partner instead of jumping a different woman every night. There was some venereal disease in the whorehouses. It came mainly from the Thai soldiers that also frequented the town. Most of the clubs would not let them in when they appeared, but we would call them over and buy them a drink whenever we could. They didn't seem to resent us too much.

A Girl Named Sue

With so many women around, I could not help but play the field if I could get away with it. That is when I met a girl named Sue. Suenee, pronounced "Sue knee," could have passed for an American girl any place in the states. We called her Sue. She had a somewhat round face that for some reason seemed out of place in Thailand. I suspected that she was half foreign, the result of a foreign tourist some nineteen years in the past.

She had a two inch scar on her cheekbone that for some strange reason made her very desirable to men. Maybe it was the extreme cuteness combined with her constant upbeat perky personality. Maybe you can equate it to times in the past when a beautiful Hollywood face was made more attractive with a mole painted on it. Sue was one of the women in the circle of friends that included my girlfriend.

They were all working girls, of course. We met at a party celebrating Sue's engagement to an American GI. He was near

the end of his tour in Thailand and ready to leave. He had ex-
tended his tour; the paper work for an American to marry a
Thai woman took some time. I suspect that the powers-that-be
made the process long in hopes that the GI would change his
mind if the woman was a working girl. I soon found out why
he would never change his mind.

My girl, Sue, with her man and I, made a trip to Bangkok
and a tourist beach in southern Thailand during a rare four-
day day weekend. Sue and I was able to interact and we became
very attracted to each other. When we returned to Korat, we
got a chance to meet often.

It was common for working girls to continue working their
clubs when they had a man in their life but they would not
take men for sex. They would serve drinks and dance with the
GIs thereby letting the real working girls have more "tricks."
They did this for several reasons.

Faithfulness to their friends, faith to Mamasan, or they
may have owed money to Mamasan. Some were unwilling to
go cold turkey when it came to giving up the life. My girl also
worked the club as money was short and they did earn very
well doing what they did.

I would join her at the club a few nights a week and get
drunk along with everyone else. Sue and I flirted a lot when
we could and I began to tease her about only having one man
in her sex life for the rest of her days. Like me, Sue was one of
those prostitutes that loved and needed lots of sex.

We eventually got around to arranging a meeting at her
place. We stayed sober on the night of the tryst to get the most
out of it. Thailand is near the equator and always very warm. It
was dark when we got there and as was the custom, we stripped
down and started taking a Thai shower.

Sue dumped buckets of water over our standing figures. The water was cool and a little shocking to the system. Sue was very aggressive and while dumping the water, she was playing with my penis to get it as large and hard as it could be, she knew what she was doing and was good at it too.

She gently pushed me back into a low railing that was the height of my ass and mounted my cock like a saddle. Like I said, my body was a little cool and when my penis entered her hot "love canal," still at body temperature, I damn near lost my load. She was in charge and played my cock to her maximum pleasure. I hung on, enjoying the show as she used me until I couldn't resist letting go myself. Wow, what a ride. Sue eventually got married and left Thailand with her husband. I never heard from her again.

About two days after Sue and I did our thing, my ass began to really hurt. It seems as though that railing Sue used as a backstop for her pleasure was rough sawn teak wood. I must have had at least two dozen festering slivers just under my skin. Teak wood was about the only wood the Thai people use for building and the human body does not like it.

I told my girlfriend that I fell against the walls in my shower at my quarters. Not suspecting a thing, she picked the slivers out and put something on my skin. I told Sue about it and she could not stop laughing. We had to stop looking at each other for fear of being confronted with, "What's the joke?"

I was assigned to the 697th Engineer Company in the 44th Engineer Group. My duties were in the Group Personnel Office. In one incident, the town of Nakhon Ratchasima outside our base caught fire. As the buildings were made with mostly teak lumber and not much separation between houses, the fire was very hot and spreading out of control. The local fire department was a joke.

In a city of tens of thousands, they had a five-hundred gallon pumper with a hand crank siren. The mayor called the US Army for help. My unit was a pipeline company and built pipelines and fuel storage tanks for the US Air Base. We had lots of pumps and pipe. The town centered round a long narrow lake filled with trash, to include human waste and lots of snakes. These snakes were not the safe type either.

We set up to pump water out of the lake into the local fire truck and two very large trucks from the air base. We had trouble priming the pump and it seemed to take hours to get it running to pump water. Meanwhile, the fire was getting huge. A Thai general from their base attempted to use explosives to stop the fire and made it worse. The local population surrounded the lake to watch our progress. There were thousands of them and as it was their town on fire, they were eerily silent.

Sometime in the middle of the night we determined we had to raise the suction pipe which stuck out into the pond and make it longer. Two volunteers floated the necessary gear out into the pond to do the work and several others went to keep the snakes away. They attached the pipe, cleared out of the pond and gave the signal to start the pump. When the water shot out of the stand pipe, it was the middle of the night. The crowd started cheering and dancing. They started bringing food and drinks to the men on the pumps. The area that burnt was about ten square blocks.

In 1966, before my one year tour was completed, I was told my first wife was in jail, our son, Greg was in foster care, and I should return to have him returned to me. I managed to take a long leave between assignments. I got a job on the green chain in a local lumber mill to earn enough money to buy a 1960 Chevrolet Bel Air sedan.

I was to report to the Personnel Management School at Fort Ben Harrison, Indiana. While I went to school, my wife and the boys stayed with friends we met in Alaska in Des Moines, Iowa. She and I had four boys in our little family now. I allowed $100 for gas from Oregon to Indiana and on to Fort George Meade, Maryland, for my final assignment.

I spent about one year at Fort Meade. We enjoyed rides around the countryside and picnics in the local parks. We did drive to our nation's capital once but the traffic kept us from trying that trip again. We did not have a lot of money so I went to work at the NCO club on base. It was evening and weekend work. I could see that I had to get on with my career so I volunteered for Viet Nam again. My assignment to Fort Meade was a dead end job.

Because of the nature of my job in the military, I was able to keep on the move and was able to go many more places than others. I was volunteering for short tours to get away from my second wife also but it was terribly irresponsible of me. Life in the military is hard on the soldier but it is also a hardship for the other family members. Separation goes both ways and the wife is left to raise the kids alone. I needed to get away from my wife but when I was separated, I did not do well. I missed her and the kids terribly.

In 1967 I received orders for assignment to the 697th Personal Service Company in Fort Bragg, NC. The unit was alerted for assignment to Viet Nam but as Thailand was in the

Viet Nam theater of operations, that is where we were going; right back to the base I was assigned to in 1965. My wife and I drove back to Oregon to get the family settled in so I could serve my tour. Again, they stayed in Tillamook. We made the trip in a 1964 Ford station wagon that we bought in Maryland. While assigned to the unit in North Carolina and before we departed overseas, I was promoted to Staff Sergeant (SSG), E-6.

Having been to Thailand on a previous tour, I was very popular especially when it came to briefings about the sex life. One night at the NCO club on Fort Bragg, I was approached by an oriental woman. She asked if I was one of those guys going to Thailand and if I was the one who had been there before.

"Yes. Why do you ask?"

She explained that her husband was in the Special Forces and had been in Thailand about two months. He had been explaining how hard life was there and she wanted to know if things others had told her were true.

"What other things?"

"The sex, you dummy," she replied.

I explained I did not want to get a fellow GI in trouble. She grinned and told me if I would come to her home and tell her stories, she would screw my brains out.

Her turnabout thinking was fair play. She declared that she was horny as hell and was not going to wait ten more months for a good licking and dicking. So, every two or three days she and her horny neighbor would pick up me and another friend of mine and take us to her house and sex out her revenge.

I was starting to get the hang of the sex thing and she knew how to make a man last. It went on for a couple of months.

We decided that the two children she had should not become accustomed to my presence, so we broke it off.

After about six months at Fort Bragg, transport to Thailand was by way of a troop ship named the USS Upshur. The trip started in Oakland Army Terminal, Oakland, California and took thirty-four days with stops in Okinawa and Vietnam. One of the pastimes of an administrative company is the ability to play pinochle. Rather than stare at open water, we played as much as twelve hours a day for at least thirty-three of those thirty-four days. We became very good at the game and for many years, I rarely lost a game.

The ship stopped at Okinawa and we were bussed to the local NCO club for a short stint on shore. The ship was carrying some unit to be assigned there. We were not allowed alcohol on the ship so drinks at the club were very welcomed.

One of the members of my unit was a staff sergeant, who was an infantryman and in the battle to take Okinawa from the Japanese during WWII. He was seventeen at the time of the battle and showed us the beach he landed at. It was a chilling experience for him and he was silent for a long time after seeing the battle sites for the first time in twenty-two years.

After my arrival in Thailand, I took a night job as assistant manager at the enlisted men's club to earn a little extra money. While on duty one night, someone or something blew up a bunker in our ammo dump filled with five-hundred pound bombs. When the explosion hit, approximately fifty people froze in place. The explosive concussion flipped the ceiling tiles and a lot of dust began to fall. That's when everyone panicked and ran for the door.

A woman went into labor; the cashier left the cage with an open door and several thousand dollars on the counter; a soldier tried to dive through a plate glass door and was bleeding heavily, and several people were trampled and hurt. I just stood in one place and watched it unfold. I usually don't panic but I felt overwhelmed that night. We eventually got control of the situation.

At the ammo dump an officer spotted a man standing frozen in the open. He spoke to him and getting no answer reported later that he thought the man was in shock. He walked up to him and, asking if he was all right, placed his hand on the man's shoulder. The blast had passed the man so fast, it crystallized his body! Much like you push a straw threw a potato. The man was dead of course. There were three others in the bunker and no trace of them was ever found. All they found of the semi-truck and trailer unloading bombs was a six inch piece of axle.

There was a lot of military action in northern Thailand as the US Military crossed borders to chase down the Viet Cong. As for my actions in the part of the country I was in, not any to speak of. The Army roll was to support the Air Force and their strikes against the enemy. The Army had it easy.

I drank a lot during my second tour in Thailand. My favorite bourbon was I. W. Harper. It only came in quarts at a cost of about $3.95. Up until my time in Thailand, I did not know any alcoholic beverage came in quart size bottles, the industry favored fifths size bottles. It may have been something to do with the military requirements of things shipped to the war effort. I could drink most of a bottle and still function. As I became older, I realize what an immature action it was.

The House Girl

We had the luxury of house girls in Thailand. They kept our quarters clean, made the beds, did the laundry and made life easy for us. I was in quarters with three other NCO's split with a common bathroom and another large room with four more men. Our house girl was a perky little 20-year-old and not the best housekeeper, but sufficient. I was the youngest NCO of the group at 24-years-old and spoke the language fairly well.

We flirted a lot, when alone, of course. Generally, we left the house girls alone sexually and some of them were married to Thai military men on that countries air base that adjoined ours.

Our house girl's name was Pluum. Pronounce the "uu" just like a "u" and you got it. The flirting started getting a little more serious. Pluum said she heard Americans liked to "jupe hee" which translates to "kiss pussy." I told her it was more like "kin hee" which means "eat pussy." That got her excited so she asked me if I would do it to her. She came from a good family and of course was not a prostitute at all. It would have been disgraceful for her to even be seen by family or acquaintances with a GI in town in any capacity.

I don't think any man would ever get tired of being propositioned. Being ever afraid of rejection, I found it almost impossible to ask just any woman for sex, prostitutes being the exception. It is so exuberant when a woman finds me attractive enough to ask me for sex. I still did not have a lot of confidence in myself due to my upbringing. So, here was a cute little woman who was probably a virgin and she wanted my tongue in her pussy and I am sure she knows what comes next.

She was small for a Thai girl and just a little plump. I was sure in view of the size of my penis that penetrating her was going to be a dramatic event for her vagina. My penis is not a record breaker, but I am proud to say that it is average-large.

We agreed to meet after dark one evening in Korat. She pulled up in a covered Pedi cab that had a privacy curtain so you could not see who was riding inside. I kept telling myself how cute she was with her pouty lips and breasts that came to a point without a bra, and that little baby fat I seem to be attracted to.

Honestly, I could not believe my luck. I was glad she chose me for this adventure. She took us to an off street establishment that really looked like an American motel. There were about three cars there. I did not know places like this existed and I believe it was one of those places that did not cater to the GI sex trade; rather its clientele was made for the upper crust when they wanted privacy. Pluum handled the office and led me to one of the units.

Thai women are very clean and always smell nice. She was wearing a sarong wrap and blouse. Since we were alone and had no fear of someone walking in on us, we got down to business in earnest. We would always joke that there were no virgins in Asia. She was so small and tight that I could not tell, and would not know, the difference as I had never penetrated a virgin before.

A Wild Night

While working at the enlisted club, I met a British corporal from India. In the American army, a corporal would be an E-4 and would have to use the enlisted club rather than the

NCO club. A corporal in the British army is a real trained fighting machine and should have been able to use the other facilities. I offered to take him to town and show him the sex trade in Thailand.

We went to Korat and I took him to the Coconut Grove Club. It was a whorehouse on an island with a fifty foot bridge over the water for access. It was gated at one end of the bridge. It had also, been off limits to American personnel for years.

We went in and asked the madam who ran the house to run the Thai soldiers off. When she asked why, we told her we were going to buy the whole house for the whole night. The club was filled with about eight privates. We bought a round of drinks to sooth their feathers and that seemed to calm them down.

The Thai soldiers would avoid the clubs filled with Americans as the price of sex and drinks were too high. They only got a few dollars a month. Even with cheaper prices at their clubs, they could only afford a prostitute about once a month. Their best bet was to make friends with American GIs and frequenting one of our clubs, play the game.

We were very loose with our money and knowing their situation many a time we would pay a prostitute or two a bunch of money to take several Thai soldiers upstairs thus getting them out of our hair. After they got what they wanted, they usually left. I guess you could say that neither one of us was stupid.

We were very drunk and my friend had a pocked full of money. I told him to pay the lady so we could get down to business. She locked the gate so we could get started. We vowed to screw every whore in the place and we did. We would go room to room to accomplish our task, there were about six or so.

We had a good supply of bourbon with us. The ladies of the house and even the madam let themselves drink more than usual and a good time was had by all. We tipped the ladies when their madam wasn't looking (she always took half or more) and left early in the morning.

I'm sure we napped for a while and we were drunker when we left than when we arrived. My buddy and I met at the enlisted club on base the next night and he told me he had to carry me for a while when we left the Coconut Grove club. He had no trouble doing so as he was a really big guy.

Of course we could not let the story of two drunk soldiers from different countries teaming up and taking over a whorehouse pass without juicing it up with consequences. About three days into a horrific hangover, I discovered that I had the clap or VD or whatever you want to call it. Late on the same day, my commanding officer called me to his office to meet a gentleman Red Cross. I felt the inevitable cold feeling run up my spine when he told me that I had to go home on emergency leave.

5

BREAK IN SERVICE

After about eight months in Thailand I received word that my wife just could not handle the job of four boys alone. I could see her point. Four boys at our age thrown together by combination from four marriages was quite a job. We were only 25-years-old. In September 1968, I was released from the Army by way of a hardship discharge.

I was very apprehensive about not being in the military. In the service, someone is responsible for all aspects of your life. If there is a problem, any problem at all, there is an answer and someone to help. Sometimes, as a leader myself, I would be responsible for the men under my control. As a civilian, I was now responsible for myself and my family. We were on our own. Scared would have been the best expression of how I felt.

I went to work for the Tillamook Farmers Co-op. My job entailed working the gas pumps; sales of farm supplies and hardware; selling automotive tires and batteries as well as installing them, driving a fuel truck and delivering fuel; delivering farm supplies to the dairy farms in the area. At times,

I worked for the Co-op, Birdseye Foods and drove trucks for two contract milk haulers, three jobs at once.

I was hired at Birdseye Foods as a tractor driver until I got one of the large tractors stuck. They then decided to take advantage of my leadership abilities from the Army and put me in charge of night irrigation crews. Driving milk trucks for the contract haulers was a very prestigious job only given to me up to that time. The owners had to drive seven days a week until they decided to trust me.

My job was to drive to various dairy farms in Tillamook and Lincoln County to pick up milk and drive it to the Tillamook Cheese Factory. Every other Saturday my milk run took me to Lincoln City. I stopped at a restaurant in Taft and Jessie's mother was working there. Anything dealing with Jessie and our time together would always get my heart beating faster. I was too scared or embarrassed to ask her mother where Jessie was. I knew she was married and had a child. It would have been nice just to know how she was doing and where she was.

In July of 1969, my first and only daughter Lorrie was born. When they announced, "It's a girl!" I felt a tremendous joy compared to when you're first born arrives. I was there in the hospital when she was born. Finally, after four boys, I had a daughter.

Scrawny

We managed to get a state GI loan and buy a house on about two acres on Latimer Road near the Tillamook Cheese Factory. I was searching for any way to make money or save money so I looked into raising chickens, ducks, geese, pigeons, calves and I even took a sheep in for labor I had done. I bought a flock of chickens for meat and eggs and wanting to raise more. So, I got a rooster to keep them fertile.

A friend told me I needed another rooster so he gave me one he had rescued. I knew it was a joke when he arrived and unloaded the bird from its transport cage. The rooster's beak was offset and looked like a pair of crossed fingers. He was blind in one eye, stone deaf and had feet that looked like two broken, worn out brooms. He managed to walk and run on those clubbed feet but would trip on them about every fourth step. Most of his tail feathers were gone or broken.

He managed to keep track of things around him by cocking his head from side-to-side and I think he could feel vibrations through his feet if he was standing still. That alone came in handy when the other rooster would charge him from time to time to exert his dominance in the flock and to keep him away from the twenty-five other hens (which he would chase) that we had. We let them run loose to supplement their food and make the eggs taste better. We called him Scrawny, for good reason. He was a mess.

On one occasion, I came around the corner of the house to find Scrawny coming toward me. He cocked his head to get a look at who it was, jumped in the air and promptly turned and ran into the side of the building. He rolled down the dirt bank sloped against the foundation, turned his good eye at me again, jumped into the air and ran into the side of the building again. By the time he landed the second time, I was laughing so hard I must have sounded like one of the hens.

He stood his ground. I would guess waiting for me to make the next move. I stood still waiting for him to leave before he killed himself. He managed to get it right the third time and left in the opposite direction.

We also had a flock of ducks, less than a dozen. By chance we had an odd number so one of the hens had no mate. She became quite gregarious with the other drakes and naturally their hens would chase her off. We could see the lone hen's frustration for lack of a mate building up and it wasn't long before she took note of the activities of Scrawny and his attempts to breed the other chickens. Their interactions were mostly half-hearted: I wouldn't want to say there were full out propositions or attempted rape on one side or the other until events came to pass; we could not fully explain with any certainly.

I remember it was mid-morning and from inside the house I heard a commotion outside. I had created a shallow pond of sorts for the ducks. It was about ten by fifteen feet and only a foot or so deep. We let the rain fill it and it would last a few days. The ducks loved it. I heard the ducks, chickens and geese all speaking their language in a loud manner at the same time.

When I got outside the ducks and geese were gathered around the pond and a few chickens were in the area. The lone duck hen had Scrawny by the neck and was attempting to drag him into the deeper end of the pond. He was all wet and looked much worse than normal, lacking a lot of feathers anyway.

Scrawny's voice was always strange, probably due to his deformed beak. He truly was showing his disdain for water and whatever his imagination was telling him about upcoming events. It's only conjecture, but I believe the lone hen was attempting to breed with him. With his clubbed feet, his attempts to escape were almost fruitless. He was covered with mud except for his head, which was bald anyway.

Some of the other ducks joined the fray and Scrawny made his escape. I reached the pond about then and most of the birds scattered. The show was over. We had some linemen working on the edge of our property and one of them had climbed a pole. He was about seventy-five feet away and from his perch laughing. He told me we must have something in our water.

Family Dynamics

In 1970, I had to give up custody of Greg to his grandparents. My wife just could not accept him. Some women and men just cannot accept another's child to raise as their own. The stepfather that raised my sister and I had this problem and to a point, so did I. I did try to not let it show with my two stepsons.

Over the years, my wife would ask me if I blamed her for giving Greg up. As usual, as not to set her off, I would say of course not. But she could have tried harder. Greg suffered greatly under his birth mother's care again as that is where he ended up. He was a good kid and his intelligence was apparent.

In 1971, we were struggling financially. I worked for my mother-in-law's husband at a Union 76 station in Beaverton, Oregon. My wife called the local army recruiter and found out that I could get back into the army as an E-6, the pay grade I was discharged with. I jumped at the chance and rejoined the Army in February. I enlisted for Alaska. Pay had gone up considerably and life was looking good. I was processed at Fort Lewis, Washington for about two months and sent to Alaska without the family, to join me later.

6

BACK IN ALASKA

Upon my arrival in Fort Richardson, Alaska, I spent that summer catching every fish in Alaska twice with a good friend, Andy. We probably threw back more fish than most men catch in a lifetime. We were both that good at knowing what to throw at the fish to get their attention. I lost track of Andy and cannot locate him.

It was a fun time for me even if I was away from my family. We did a little drinking too. We would spend the day fishing and on the drive home we would try to hit every bar we could just to say we did it. On one occasion, Andy lost his truck and camper to another friend in a game of dice at a bar in Anchorage. He won it back before the night was over. From then on he asked me not to let him get too drunk.

The winter of 1970-71 was a record snowfall year; spring was late in coming due to all the snow it had to melt. Andy and I drove his camper to Jerome Lake on the Seward Highway. There was a small undeveloped pull-out with a few other fishermen there. We set up and proceeded to drill a hole for fishing.

The ice was almost six feet thick. The other fishermen were fishing their holes but no one was catching anything. We broke through the ice and within a few minutes caught our first rainbow trout. Apparently we had drilled over an underwater channel and spent a couple of hours catching eighteen fish. We kept them alive in a surface pond and switched smaller ones for the bigger ones as we caught them. The limit was ten each.

Everyone left except two sergeants major from our base. We would have shared the hole but Andy discovered on a coffee run to the truck that they had thrown their trash over the bank and we assumed they were going to leave it. They left so we caught our last two fish and sacked out for the night. This story is about what happened the next day.

We left Jerome Lake with twenty trout, all of which were over twenty-two inches. We laid them out on newspaper on the camper floor to keep them cold as we had no cooler. It was still winter anyway. We were both out of money and near out of gas, but Andy had a gas credit card so we stopped in Girdwood for fuel.

In those days there wasn't much self-service at gas stations. They checked oil, water and washed your windshield. As the owner was performing his chores, I had the back of the camper open for some reason. The owner spied the fish on the floor and exclaimed how he was too busy running his business to go fishing. He said it had been years.

"I sure miss the taste of fresh trout," he stated.

Andy overheard him and as we were out of beer and money to buy any, he offered to slide three of the trout under the counter if a six-pack of Bud were to fall on the camper floor.

When the owner returned to his duties, Andy told me to take six of the trout inside as we didn't need that many anyway.

"Besides, he said, "I would kill for a beer right now and six trout is worth it."

We finished up at the gas station and drove off. A mile or so down the road we stopped to claim our prize. We opened the camper door and there were two six-packs of beer! I guess both parties placed a higher price on their wishes than their possessions.

I flew to Oregon in September and my family of six drove up the Alcan Highway in a 1967 Mercury Comet station wagon. It is a good thing the kids were small. The trip took five or six days. In those days, the Alcan Highway consisted of over 1000 miles of gravel roadway. It still had the twists and turns from its construction.

In the winter of 1972, my wife's mother and her husband, Slim, came up for a visit. I took Slim ice fishing at Big Lake. My favorite spot was off the shoreline of a well-known bar. It was good for a few drinks and a warm place to come to.

They were collecting fish for a fish fry in the spring so we would give them the smaller ones when we were finished catching. The ice had become too thick for my auger so I went to the car and got an axe. Slim and I worked on a hole big enough to get in to work the auger down farther.

The hole we axed out was about five feet in diameter and about eighteen inches deep when the inevitable happened. I should have known better. Anyone should know you can't dig a hole in the water. The top of the ice was the water level. When the auger broke through, Slim and I were kneeling instantly in eighteen inches of water and the ambient air temperature was about fifteen degrees. By the time we traveled the two-hundred or so feet to the bar, everyone was laughing and told us they kept the fire hot. They knew what was going to happen even if I had forgotten.

Only people who have been to Alaska can know the calm of a June or July morning, around two or 3am. It is bright daylight all night. You have to wonder how something so big can be so quiet. You can see mountains a hundred and fifty miles away but you can't hear a thing; maybe just a whiney mosquito or a fly nearby looking for a patch of skin, probably yours.

In the summer of 1973, I was sitting in the middle of a small lake on Fort Richardson. I usually go catching on these small lakes but that was not the day; I was only fishing. I had my oldest son with me and he wasn't having much luck either. We did hear a moose bottom feeding on some aquatic plant across the lake. Every time she came up to chew, you could hear the water running off her soaked and shiny head.

At the other end of the lake I saw a beaver swimming silently. The sun was beating down at the low summer angle and reflecting off the water. The only wind was that which came off those pesky mosquito's wings. It was barely hot. The military recreational activities service rented boats from a small shack on the shore to military personnel and their dependents. It was staffed by a young man who had to be bored out of his mind having to sit there all night, all summer. As it was a hot night, he was sitting on a chair propped against the building.

The rental boat was aluminum which meant we had to tread lightly or no fish would come near us. Sound would be amplified by anything hitting the side or bottom. For safety sake, the seats were built into the boat frame and hollow. I guess to serve to keep the boat afloat in the event of a spill. The seats were a little hard on your bottom and in view of what happen that day, I know we had no cushions to make them more comfortable.

I began to feel the need to pass a little gas, well, maybe a lot of gas. No big deal. Guys do it all the time, especially when you're out in the middle of nowhere and no one will know about it anyway. It might as well have been a base drum in a crowded church.

I rose up a little cheek on one side to aid its passing and let it rip. That hollow seat amplified that sound fivefold and you couldn't fool anyone as to what it was. You would have thought I was sitting on a stadium microphone the way the sound was magnified. It's a good thing environmental impact statements hadn't been invented yet or the paperwork would have sunk the boat.

The impact on the creatures around me was evident. I could hear the guy on shore laughing; I saw the moose out of the water and heading for the trees; the beaver slapped its tail and dove to wherever beavers go when surprised. My son couldn't stop giggling. I told him that was my fish caller. Since I didn't want to spend the rest of the morning in a windless purple haze, we gave it up for the day and went home. Me? I'll be fine. I just don't mix boats and beans ever again.

An old timer—let's call him as I was young then—taught me something about fishing that I have used many times over the years. The lakes of the Mat-Su Valley are mostly stocked by Alaska State Fish and Game and the fish have no place to spawn. When they introduce the fish to the lake, they do what they have been taught at the hatchery and feed on anything that hits the water. They are easy to catch and the dumb fish

are gone in the next wave of anxious fisherpersons that wet a
line. A few of the smarter (or slower) fish hang back and learn
that something hitting the water means one of your schoolmates disappear.

These fish get more cautious over time and find other ways
to feed. The way the old timer said it was, "big fish don't like
little fish except to eat." They don't like to hang out with little
fish and they certainly don't like to feed with the little guys.

A co-worker of mine from Fort Richardson and I took our
sons to Kepler-Bradly Lakes for some camping and fishing. It
was a late August weekend and the campground was crowded
with tents and tarps of hopeful fishermen. They drifted in
and out of the fishing spots on the lake and were catching
what was called the normal-sized fish for the lake about eight
to ten inches. Very rarely someone would catch a twelve inch
lunker trout. I helped my boys catch a few and my friend did
the same with his. We fried the fish up for dinner and did the
normal things people do when camping with your sons.

In late August, it starts to get very dark at night, so about
dusk I found what I thought would be a good spot on the bank
of the lake to try out the trick the old timer had informed me
of. I used a slip-line float and uncured salmon egg clusters
and cast my line out as far as I could and let the bait sit on
the bottom. I lit up a gas lantern and set it on the ground.
The light of the lantern shined across the surface of the water
and the float stood out like a flashlight. Nothing happen for
about two hours but then it was a fisherman's dream.

I caught a limit of ten trout in less than sixty minutes. The
smallest was about sixteen inches and most were twenty inches or close to it. They were all fat having entered their fall

feeding frenzy before freeze up. The best thing was that their flesh was the salmon color of healthy trout rather than the pale color of hatchery fish. I caught my last fish of the limit and all activity stopped. No bites, no fish, nothing. It was very dark so I cleaned the fish, leaving their heads on so everyone would believe their length and retired to the tent for some sleep. I hung the fish from a tent line to keep them cool.

Sometime after sunup I was awoke by a commotion outside the tent. My friend came in and told me my fish had attracted a crowd of half a dozen or so and they wanted to know where I caught those fish.

"Right down there," I told him, pointing to the lake.

"No way," they lightheartedly replied.

Using the fisherman's demeanor of tease, bluster and challenge, I told them you just have to know how to fish. I assured them that the fish were, indeed, caught in that lake in the middle of the night. We iced the fish down and went home not knowing if the others caught anything bigger or not. Life lesson: listen to those old fishermen to become a better fisherperson.

We bought a new Dodge van and had a lot of trips into Alaska camping and fishing. It was great. In December of 1973, we drove the van down the Alcan for my new assignment in Fort Campbell, Kentucky. The trip was a cold one. We left around midnight which was the earliest I could sign out from my unit. The first night we stayed in a cabin in a place called Pine Valley in the Yukon Territory (as of 2014, the cabins were still there).

It was very cold, probably thirty below. It was a one-room cabin with oil heat. We were traveling with our cat named,

Trouble. It was too cold to leave her in the van so we got permission to take her inside with us. To make it easier to travel with her, we kept her on tranquilizers.

The kids were older, bigger and wiser and with the van, the trip was rather pleasant. One memorable event was my wife having to pee, and in those days there were no rest stops for hundreds of miles so she squatted in front of the van out of sight of the kids. There was no traffic to speak of either.

The entire year of 1974, I was stationed with the 101st Airborne Division in Fort Campbell. The Viet Nam war was over and the Army had plenty of soldiers to assign all over the world. My job was the NCO In-Charge of the overseas levy section, responsible for reassigning those men and women to their new stations. The military suddenly had a lot of troops to pass around. There were so many assignments coming from Department of the Army that my section blew up from five to fifteen people within days and even then we could not keep up. We did the best we could and let the people in charge take the flak.

While assigned at Fort Campbell, the Army sent me to Advanced NCO training in Fort Ben Harrison, Indiana. This was quite an honor as it was the highest schooling an enlisted man could get in the military and meant greater things were in store for me.

We took advantage of being in Kentucky and toured a lot of Civil War battle sites. Other than that we were not too impressed with the South. After Alaska, things were just too flat. While there, we did visit my wife's sister in Florida and got to pass through several states we had not been to yet.

In 1975, I arranged a transfer to Fort Huachuca, Arizona. I did not enjoy the turmoil of my job in Fort Campbell.

Assignment to Arizona became one of the best assignments of my twenty years in the military. The whole family enjoyed exploring Arizona in a small camper. We traveled most of the state including many of the back roads, but we did not get to see the Grand Canyon.

I saw my first UFO while in Arizona. I was standing outside in my carport around 7pm. The object came out of Huachuca Canyon and made a ninety and forty-five degree turn at the same speed as a meteor. I have been in aviation and in the artillery and there is nothing man has that can duplicate the speed and maneuvers that this object performed. It made a believer out of me.

7

COMBAT ARMS

In January 1976, after a year in Arizona, the nightmare happened. I was selected to be reclassified, along with several thousand other mid-level NCOs, into the combat arms. Through upgrades in administration and improved use of computers, most of us worked ourselves out of a job in our respective career fields. Through attrition we were moved to where we were needed; where we could become relevant again and continue our military endeavors.

I was good as an administrator and enjoyed my work there. I felt abandoned by the Army when they put me in the combat arms. I spent years in the top two and a half percent in my administrative career field and due to the needs of the service, I know the reclassification was a good thing, but it still left me very hollow inside. Later, I would come to realize, it was a good move.

As far as the combat arms, I was very good at that too but anyone can excel in that field. I had fun as any man would if you gave him a 105mm Howitzer, a good crew and all the ammo you could shoot. Much later, when I made Sergeant First Class, better referred as, SFC, E-7, they gave me six guns with crews to supervise.

As a Staff Sergeant, E-6, I became Gun Chief of Base Piece in Battery "B", in an unnamed artillery battalion of the 9th Infantry Division at Fort Lewis, Washington after a six week training session. I got the job as Base Piece Chief because my gunner, whom we will call Andy, was good and a good training tool for an upcoming NCO in the artillery. Base piece does more firing than all the other guns in a battery for targeting purposes and to aim the battery before all six guns fire.

Soldiers will bitch about anything and probably pretty much everything. From chow to their leaders and everything in between, it is all wrong. Including me, the one thing that really got to everyone in my circle for my first few years in the military was guard duty.

The sergeant would form a guard squad, and with empty weapons we would march around a salvage yard full of junk vehicles and rusted out desks and file cabinets; all within strict guidelines passed down for decades from military rules and tradition. As privates, we could not understand why we had to perform this bit of harassment.

When I finally made sergeant I realized what guard duty was all about. These were the guys who would be guarding my ass in combat and if I wanted to get any sleep then they better be good at it. As a leader, bitching in front of your troops was not allowed. The alternative was to see the military reasoning behind things that may have bothered me for years and obey without question.

Bad Leadership

Now, for all you nitpickers, this next story is based on my experiences at a different time in the military so things are probably not the same for you now. Terms, regulations, training and mission are most certainly much advanced and probably better in today's Army.

Combat arms units at that time were tested for their combat effectiveness through an exercise called an ARTEP, Army Training and Evaluation Program. Word was at that time that no unit ever fails an ARTEP. It's just a test of combat effectiveness and was usually graded by peers from another like unit in the division. In other words, "Scratch my back and I'll scratch yours."

The time was used to correct little things that would affect combat effectiveness and one could always find a few things that made the show look good. What makes this story unusual is that it was an outright failure in leadership so bad, it could not be ignored.

Our battalion was scheduled to take this test at the Yakima Firing Center in central Washington State. The Battalion Commander (we will call him the CO), the Battalion Executive Officer (XO) and the Battalion Command Sergeant Major (CSM) were all "retreads", but for different reasons.

Officers at times in their careers have to come off their desk jobs and serve command time. So we got them, and their ideas of what command is, along with a CSM who was willing to enforce their ways without question or suggestion. I will never be able to explain or understand why these three knuckle-head leaders decided to attempt to lead a battalion into an ARTEP with such incompetence.

We NCOs were gathered for a briefing and told we would set up a base camp in the hills of the Yakima Firing Center, and we could not utilize the hard barracks area of the regular camp. Furthermore, we were told to go out on several practice exercises, returning after each to the base camp area and perform all duties in that area.

The hard barracks area consisted of permanent buildings, running water, mess halls, a motor pool, Base-Exchange (BX) and even an NCO club where a man could get a beer or two. But the hard barracks area would be off limits.

Then we were told that we would practice for about seven weeks and then perform our ARTEP. This meant that our soldiers would be living in the dirt for two months. The troops were to pair up and utilize their two-man pup tents, which mean they slept on the ground. The NCOs would utilize the larger eight to ten-man tents with cots. Rank has its privileges but we could see hard feelings coming with two months of this kind of living conditions.

There would not be a mess tent for meals, rather rows of standing benches out in the open. Our showers were to be supplied by a trailer full of water on a slight rise, gravity fed to a tent below and the water would be unheated. There was a regular quartermaster shower point with hot water about two miles away but for reasons never explained, it was also off limits.

The CO, XO and CSM all stayed at the hard barracks area with beds and hot showers. Every morning we were in base camp they would arrive by chopper about the same time we were having our morning meal. This meant a lot of dust and even more hard feelings. Every soldier knew where they were the night before.

Every leader knows you should drift toward the best comfort level you can for your troops, especially when you are asking them to perform duties for which you will be judged as a leader. What the three so-called leaders were asking of our men was border line punishment. Everyone could see trouble coming.

Battery commanders and officers could say nothing and senior NCOs could say very little. Driving soldiers for seven weeks practice for such a critical test is asking too much. Making matters worse, treating them as if they are being punished is just asking for trouble. They got what they asked for.

After a few weeks, the three day exercises and two or so days in camp, the rhythm began to get old. We were just practicing and that is what makes a combat unit effective when the real thing comes along. We were practicing too much and troop morale was almost nonexistent. We NCOs did our best to go along with the training regiment expected of us. I could see what the three at the top were trying to accomplish and did my best to understand, but it wasn't working for me and a lot of other mid-level NCOs.

Adding to the problem was the cold showers. Most of the men were living on the ground in those two-man tents with very little personal space. The ground space of a two-man tent is less than a four-by-eight sheet of plywood. They were eating dust when in base camp every time a chopper would land, wearing dirty clothes most of the time and told those cold showers are just fine. Luckily, the weather was rather mild. Weather in Yakima Firing Center can get brutal. I took it upon myself to try and do something.

We figured that if the powers in battalion command would not take action against the cold showers then it must be up to us. We found a deep arroyo with comparably vertical sides and wide enough to accommodate a make shift canvas and tent pole privacy shower. Using our unit's water trailer and emersion heaters, we scrounged clean garbage cans; lengths of water hose and a Number 10 can with lots of holes in it.

Emersion heaters were placed in garbage cans filled with water. When fired with diesel fuel, they do a good job of keeping water hot. We siphoned water fast enough to supply a shower head—the Number 10 can—with good and warm water. We gave our entire battery a much deserved warm shower.

Our first sergeant bragged about all the activity to the other battery first sergeants and we gave showers to their units also. They had to supply a water trailer and a little help. The battalion XO heard about it and came over to watch with my battery commander. When asked what we were doing, my commander told him that Sergeant Jennings was giving classes in field sanitation. He could say nothing but by now everyone but him found the humor in the situation.

The situation did a lot to boost morale of the entire battalion. The troops looked at it as a revenge maneuver as it made the XO look bad and his cold shower set up never was used after that. Each battery appointed an NCO to give the same class every time we were in the camp area.

The ARTEP was a miserable failure. The leaders of our battalion must have made enemies along their career path because the write up about the exercise had no praise and mentioned their failure to monitor troop morale. Within weeks the three leaders were transferred and everyone knew why. About two months later, all the battalion NCO's were called to a meeting with the new sergeant major.

"You know you're going to have to pass an ARTEP don't you?" stated the new sergeant major.

Without waiting for a response, he went on to say that we were going to go back to Yakima, but this time we will be staying in the hardened barracks area.   We will have two practiced ARTEPs. We will then perform maintenance on our equipment, and leaving the equipment, we will return the troops to Fort Lewis for a week off.

With a grin on his face, he said, "Your reputation precedes you. So when you get back to Yakima, I expect the best ARTEP ever fired." He got what he asked for.

It was during the stay in the hardened barracks area motor pool that I had a very close brush with death. One of soldiers called three of us over to the rear of his truck. We were standing between his truck and the front of another. What he wanted to show us was the newest playboy magazine centerfold and other pictures. These trucks are known as duce and a half trucks and are rather large. The tail gate was head high. The magazine was boring and on today standards would only qualify as soft porn.

"Get real. I could dream up more than that stuff," I told the guys.

Just as the last man stepped just inches from between the vehicles, the front bumper of the rear truck slammed into the tailgate of the lead vehicle and anyone standing there would have been cut in half. Another duce and a half truck had been parked up a moderate slope in the same row, loaded with heavy artillery rounds and without the parking brake set.

My gunner, Andy, and I had a reputation for taking unusual actions with exceptional results for the good of our
men and unit. During another exercise at a different time
in Yakima Firing Center, another unit was jamming our radio signals that we used to call fire missions. This was their
combat roll but they were to jam the enemy signals, not
ours and we were having a tough time completing steel on
target.

We had no defense from their actions except what we
would do in combat. Additionally, we were in practice roll
with camouflage nets and all the accruements a combat unit
would use to avoid detection from the enemy. This commu-
nications "jamming" unit was sitting on top of a hill with no
effort in hiding from anyone.

Andy and I asked the first sergeant for permission to do
something about the situation. He gave us the usual speech
that he did not want to hear what we purposed; did not want
us to destroy any government property, "and for God's sake,
don't hurt anyone."

After a night with no moon and heavy cloud cover, the
power cables leading from the generators (shut down for the
night) to the communication equipment of a certain signal
company parked on top of a hill somehow became disconnect-
ed and rolled into a deep canyon. They must have gotten the
message as we had no more trouble. Andy and I, as was our
usual custom, did not take the credit. Our reputation would
not allow that.

Speaking of our reputation, when soldiers go to the field
for maneuvers and/or training, there is one universal problem. They get sluggish after a few days. This is mostly caused
by the fact that there is no place to "take a dump." They don't

provide bathrooms when you move so much and so expeditiously. I have seen these soldiers hold it beyond two weeks.

We always knew when we were to go out on training missions and how long. Andy and I always liked to take a variety of treats to make life better. Things like jerky, pepperoni, canned meats, candy, and dried fruit snacks. Our men never seemed to get the hint to bring their own stuff; electing instead to bum off of Andy and I. Our men had a reputation for always showing an overabundance of energy during training. I'm sure it had a lot to do with all the prunes we gave them as that is all we seem to have left whenever they asked for some of our stash. Whatever works!

Korea & Sue

In December of 1977, I left for an assignment in Korea. I spent the entire year of 1978 there. It was another shock to my impression of the world. In the 1970's, many parts of Korea was still beginning to enter the modern world. A typical Korean house was built with mud bricks or if they had enough money, they used cinder blocks. The windows and sliding doors where wood framed with a sort of oiled rice paper used in place of glass. Most all of the homes and shops used a burning large charcoal brick buried in the floor along with the chimney to the outside for heat. There were many deaths each year across the country from the gasses given off through cracks in the system.

US Military bases were scattered throughout the country side. I'm sure there was a good reason for this but I did not know why. Each base had a village outside the gates and was great for the local economy. There was the usual gift shops, tailor shops, open air restaurants, and of course, the bars; lots and lots of bars.

The best part of being sent to Korea was I was back in the saddle again. Sex was cheap, safe and the pussies were small. By this time in my life, I was getting the hang of how to penetrate that little slit or what I like to call the mighty-tighty. I went with half dozen or so women and then met a girl named Sue. What first attracted me was her formidable face. She was pretty and had a slightly sad look but when you started talking to her, she was a lot of fun in addition to being smart.

The best thing was that she loved sex, but I refuse to label her a whore. She would only set herself up with a GI for the duration of his tour and when he was gone, she would get another. She did not work the whorehouses. It was a tradition in Korea to keep a picture of porn under their mattress to ensure good sex. Sue kept several pictures and they were very good. I guess it worked as she could not leave me alone and sex several nights a week was the norm. On weekends, it was expected; mornings and evenings.

Cyrus

I was promoted to Sergeant First Class (SFC), E-7 after my arrival in Korea. This meant that I joined the ranks of the senior enlisted class. About half way through my tour, I was sent home for two weeks because my real father, Cyrus Jennings, had died. I was shocked to learn that he was still alive as I had not heard anything about him for at least 30 years. I took advantage of the military policy of paid transport and emergency leave for the death of a family member. I did not go to the funeral as I did not want anything to do with the man who abandoned us so long ago. He was a nothing to me.

In December 1978, I returned to Fort Lewis and served in another artillery battalion. It was a very unpleasant assignment. My daughter was facing some severe problems so I arranged a transfer to the replacement unit on Lewis. This enabled me to spend more time with my family instead of constant trips to the field for training.

I arranged for an unaccompanied short tour in Europe in order to leave my family in one place before my retirement. It was common for the military to send soldiers nearing retirement on a long tour with their family, to entice them to stay in the service beyond their twenty year retirement eligibility date. I could not see staying beyond that date in view of my involuntary assignment to the combat arms. Little did I know what was to come as a consequence of my next assignment.

8

GREECE

I arrived in Athens, Greece during the off season for tour-
ism. I was on a military assignment to replace a First
Sergeant at a nuclear weapons storage site. Basically, we
were there to antagonize the Russians. We were guarding the
weapons and the Greeks were supposed to fire them when
needed. From what I saw of the Greek military, we were going
to hand them a bullet so they could tie it on the end of a stick
and go fishing.

The junior grades in the Greek army were supported by
their families, not the government. I believe they got about
ten dollars a month and their family had to give them any other spending money they needed. Their uniforms were hand-
me-downs from other soldiers. There was some sort of draft
or required service in effect at that time. Insubordination was
not tolerated; I saw none and don't know how they prevented
it. It was one of those things you didn't ask.

Senior enlisted were processed and briefed for about two
weeks in Athens before being sent north to their assigned
bases. As the country of Greece is about twenty-five percent

communist, we were to keep a low profile whenever possible. They made NCOs live in towns rather than the barracks. Amongst the indigenous population we wore civilian clothes, even when traveling to and from work; then they gave us rides in a military jeep. You can fill in the humor here; I am at a loss.

We were kept in a hotel in a resort town on the outskirts of Athens for the duration of our in-briefing. This was close to the American air base and even closer to the NCO club. The hotel was under contract to the US government and the staff was friendly and helpful, but I think they liked the tourist better because they tipped more. There was about ten of us and we had a lot of down time. We usually just sat around drinking or chatting about our new found adventures to come.

We were a little reluctant to venture out much in view of the warnings we had been given about some of the people. Some of their customs we would call very strange. As an example, waving to someone with an open hand like we do in western society is the equivalent of giving someone the finger in Greece. To this day whenever I get the chance and see someone I feel like insulting, like politicians, I wave as hard as I can.

Dora

I could not help thinking that the opportunities for sex could not be too great with all the commies in this country so I decided to wait and see what developed. It didn't take long and things started to look really good. All of us were sitting around the hotel lobby, for whatever reason, we had nothing to do. She came in like an actress at the Oscars, under full assault on men's minds: silent, filled with purpose, beautiful, magnificent.

Men are such fools when a woman comes into the room. They all ogle in unison and that lecherous look in itself is so obvious. I bet only one in a thousand can do a good job of ignoring the dreamed up possibilities. On the other hand, when a woman spends an hour or more getting ready for the entry into a group of men she knows is there, why is she taking the time? Is it a tease? Do you think she would pretend she would be alone and not seen? She is so good at acting like she would not be noticed. Is it a form of innocence? I think not.

Anyway, there she was, pretending like she thinks no one sees her but knowing better. I was at a low coffee table, relaxing with a deck of solitary cards. I'm the ignoring type but I know when to glance, unseen. She said something to the bartender and slowly walked in my direction. She was all woman, all knowing, and not innocent nor filled with a confident purpose. Somehow, I knew that I was her target. Her actions were too direct. I suppose this scenario is what the other oglers were hoping for but I was the chosen one.

"Would you like to play with me?" she purred.

I'm kind of fast on the tongue and her comment was just asking for my retort. "It depends on how the deck is stacked," I answered, deliberately in a low whisper.

My low volume meant she had to lean over to ask what I had said. I know it was as intentional as my low voice for her to let me get a good look at her chesty attributes. My feelings about the female breast is if you can't touch, why look? Staring is strictly forbidden because it puts the woman in charge. I don't mind letting the fairer sex take the lead, it has its uses.

Speaking of uses, I knew I was being used but I was very suspicious. In view of our sensitive assignment, being in a strange country, and the beauty and boldness of this woman, I felt that this could lead to almost anything. Is she a prostitute?

I decided to throw caution to the wind and let her lead me around a while and see if there was anything in this for me. If she asks for money I could always give a polite no. If she asked me any sensitive questions, maybe I could lead her on for a while past a physical pleasurable moment or two; or, I would just tell her I was a cook and didn't know anything.

We made a lot of small talk and had a few drinks. I bought a round and she would buy two. Drinks in Athens are expensive but money seemed no problem with her. For a while I thought maybe she was a sexually frustrated housewife.

She said she was Greek, and at that time I had no reason to doubt her. Her intelligence was apparent in her conversation and she spoke fluently about many subjects. She seemed very honest in her opinions. I still thought I was being played for something, but what? If this was a seduction, why choose me? I may be a handsome army sergeant but with all the men in the world chasing the mighty-tighty, she seemed to have a bull's eye on me. Well, what the hell. I might as well sacrifice my body and play along.

She invited me to her room to help her take a bath. The sex was outstanding but I only have two grades of sex: fantastic and outstanding. We had a great time for several days. I would write about it but it is not relevant at this time and you probably already know how it is done. We went out to eat at the NCO club a few times and explored Glifada, which is the section of Athens we were staying in. I love intelligent women, and she was a shiner; throw in her very aggressive sex and she was really something. Her name was Dora.

My indoctrination in Athens was finished and the powers-that-be, released me for travel to Kilkis in the north central part of the country. I could travel any way I wish with the travel allowance they gave me. Dora offered to pay for a taxi if I would take her. It was three hundred miles. The cost didn't seem to bother her. I had fleeting thoughts of being kidnapped. What a way to go.

When we got to Kilkis, Dora stayed in a hotel while I reported in. I rented a villa from an elderly couple. They were the in-laws of one of the soldiers on the base. He was the only GI I knew of that married a local woman. We were given a substantial housing and food allowance to live on the local economy, so I set up housekeeping and Dora moved right in.

She began to act a little strange within days. She would knit all day and get on me for being late to come home. My job comes first and I told her so. She would laugh things off as if it appeared she was on the wrong track. She would disappear every two weeks or so for about three days and come back with a bag full of drachmas (Greek money). She wanted sex every day and I didn't find that strange or unpleasant. That's why I put up with her attempt to be bitchy.

She bought several appliances and furniture for prices unheard of in the US, at least four times as much. She paid $100 for a simple blender. The excess was all taxed. I suspected her of acting the way she did to set me off and talk about work and why I was late. I said nothing. Dora even accused me of having a male lover on the base. After a few months of this charade, she went away and never came back. I sold the stuff she bought for a lot of drachmas as there is quite a black market in Greece to avoid taxes.

Texas, Greece

We were an artillery detachment in possession of nuclear weapons. We were the front lines of the Cold War. As I have stated before, our mission in addition to guarding the weapons was to antagonize the Russians by just being there. That is my opinion; my pay grade would not let me think of anything beyond that.

Because of the importance that the United States government placed on what we were doing there, in their opinion, we were constantly barraged with very important persons, or VIP's. There were times we hosted some really high-level VIP's. They claimed to be worried about our morale but their showing up created such fervor that it did more to destroy it. Some did enjoy a visit from the Dallas Cowgirls. We numbered about thirty men and I was the acting first sergeant. My clerk and I were from Oregon and our detachment commander was a Texan.

Troop morale is the responsibility of the officers and NCOs in any unit so we decided to write each of the state's governor's offices for a state flag. We hoped to get them all and display them in our lounge. My clerk and I challenged the commander to a race between the arrival of our state flag and his.

We received word of a very busy day. Three different choppers with some kind of brass were expected. As usual, due to the distance from Athens they could not give us a sequence or time of arrival. One was some Navy captain and had something to do with a nuclear warhead. I don't remember the second and the third was the Sergeant Major of the Army.

The Sergeant Major of the Army was the most powerful enlisted man in the US Army and could even have influence on an officer's career. When new officers get their training they are told that they are responsible for their command, but their NCO is in charge. This sergeant major had my commander very nervous. I should have been but my morale was in the basement. I knew that due to the distance from command, big wigs had no place to stay and did not want to stay on the ground too long. He would be gone in a flash.

The mail truck arrived and what was the usual case, several of us were standing by the vehicle to see what mail we would get. As luck would have it, there was a package from Texas and I knew it was not a beef steak. Some of the guys started teasing my clerk and I. Someone asked how to tell the commander he won the contest. One of the guys said to run the flag up the flag pole with the stars and stripes we flew daily.

"Who would do that?" someone asked.

"Oh yeah, I'll do it!" I found myself saying.

What did I have to lose? Being the first sergeant I only had to answer to one other in the detachment. I tied the Texas flag under the US Flag and ran it up the pole again. I walked away wondering how I would attract the commander's attention to his trophy.

Within moments, there was the *giddy-wop, giddy-wop* of an approaching chopper. The commander ran out of the orderly room and called for me to meet him at the chopper pad. It seemed so unnecessary to call for me as the orderly room, flag pole and chopper pad were all within such a small space.

As the engine powered down, the Sergeant Major of the Army and his aide, a master sergeant, stepped out. They saluted my commander and the captain introduced me. Looking up at the flag pole, the sergeant major asked the commander, "What's with the Texas flag, Captain?"

Most officers I have known were not easily rattled. The captain looked up at the flags and then at me and I could see he was in a state of panic. Remember, he is responsible but I am in charge of everything that happens on our small post. He told me later he figured I had something to do with it.

"I ran it up this morning, sergeant major," I announced before my commander could.

Now the captain looked really mad and I was beginning to get a little worried about my own ass and my next efficiency report. This was becoming very embarrassing for all of us. The Sergeant Major of the Army and our American flag were two things not to be joking with.

"How did you know I was from Texas?" the sergeant major asked, with a big grin on his face and reaching to shake my hand.

The transition from panic to anger and now to relief must have been really hard for an officer that did not like to show emotion often and all within under a minute. After what we had just been through, the sergeant major's next statement didn't really matter much.

"You should know that the Texas flag is upside-down."

I bought an old VW Beetle from a departing GI and had the engine rebuilt. I then sold it for a good profit. All this so I could pay for my mid-tour leave to visit family. The cheap flights were booked up so the travel agency I was using arranged an unusual way to get me to the states.

I had to fly to Rome, Zurich, Frankfurt, Atlanta and then Seattle but the price was within my means. While in Rome, I met an oil field worker from the US who had been working in Saudi Arabia. I was in uniform and he bought me a drink.

I returned the favor handing the bartender a twenty dollar bill. He gave me 4000 Italian Lira as change. I thought I made out pretty good so I asked how much it was worth. Another drinker at the bar told me it was worth about two American dollars. My first thought was to give the foreign money to my kids and then I realized I had just paid eighteen dollars for two drinks. That was expensive on 1980 standards. I don't remember what I did with the change.

In June of 1981, half way through my twelve month tour, I was transferred to Drama, again in Northern Greece but nearer to Turkey and the Mediterranean Sea. One of the men on base informed me of a room for rent in town, as was required of senior NCOs. The Greek landlord also ran a little cigarette/candy shop on the ground floor below the room.

The rent was very reasonable and the man was so friendly I couldn't help but rent it. We became close friends, mostly because of our penance to laugh at almost anything and he liked the fact that I would bring bourbon home all the time. It's never good to drink alone. His name in Greek was too long so I just called him Bud; he liked that. He told me to watch out for some of the women in the building but didn't tell me why. I found out when one of them propositioned me in the elevator.

A sex addict will accept an invitation from anyone at any time but I just could not do this one. I don't mind large women but she was shaped like a turnip, nodules and all. She was not ugly but close. I believe ugly is in actions, not looks. She had a mustache and had a faint smell I could not identify. She was with a very beautiful, slender, pretty-young girl who had to interpret for her as she spoke not one word of English. The girl was her granddaughter, about twenty, I guessed. How do you say awkward? Even if she was sexually approachable, how could I tell her granddaughter, "Sure, tell her I'll do her?"

I was 38-years-old, in my prime and I guess handsome in most quarters. What was this woman thinking? She probably figured, "you will never get any if you don't ask."

I'm not arrogant but, yes, ok, I admit, she was ugly! Later, I had fleeting thoughts of six more months left on my tour without sex but no, no, no, forget that. I managed to smile at her when we occasionally crossed paths in the halls and avoid her attempts for conversation. She was persistent if nothing else.

I told Bud about the solicitation and jokingly asked him why he couldn't control his women, teasing him for not giving them enough of his time. He knew who she was and told me she was quite a ride.

"Would you like sloppy seconds?" he asked.

I turned him down of course. I guess he got me back on that one. I didn't know if he was serious or not. I guess you would call that back and forth a sample of the crude teasing men do to each other.

Bud called me down one day and told me he knew a woman that wanted to meet me. I asked if it was the big one's sister.

"No, get serious. She is very nice."

At that time, any woman would do just to get the "turnip" off of me. Thus, began a very sad chapter in our lives.

Dot

We hit it off right away. She was attractive, very shy; spoke just a little English and my age too. She had a job in re-forestation for the government somewhere in the wilds of Greece. She would be gone about five to ten days and come back with just enough money to live on for the rest of the month. I was immediately attracted to her. Her name was Dorothy and of course, I called her Dot for short.

We had a lot of off time on our hands in Greece. The job called for some very intense and serious operations, be it moving a nuclear weapon or communication war games on a worldwide secure network. Most often, we just vegetated and worked on our morale. Dot and I spent a few days getting to know each other.

As a senior NCO, I was required to provide for myself for housing and meals. Just walking the streets and taking in all the shops was about all there was to do most of the time. We ate out a lot at the local taverns as they were called. There was lots of good Greek food and drink and it was a pleasant pass time, very romantic in the Greek summer.

Once I had to go to Athens for something, I don't remember what it was. We took the bus as I wanted to see more of the Greek countryside. We could have flown if I chose to. In Athens, she introduced me to some of her family. She had property there but it was damaged by an earthquake and un-livable at that time.

Her family consisted of her brother, his wife and they had two children in their 20's still living with them. This was usually the custom as they were still working on their education and the cost of living in Greece could get very expensive if you had no job. Jobs were scarce. Dot's brother owned a barber shop and was doing well.

While Dot was away working, her brother drove me all over Athens to show me the sights. Her nephew was in the process of buying a Honda 250 motorcycle. I asked him how much and in drachmas, he said $22,000.00. I said he had to be wrong but he showed me the financing paper work and it was indeed that amount. Twenty thousand of it was in taxes! Any new car was in excess of $100,000 drachmas.

A used car had a better tax break and only the rich could afford new. The Greeks would keep their cars running forever if possible. Most of the taxis were Mercedes sedans or American cars from the 50's. That says a lot for the socialist government of Greece that they had at the time.

Sex with Dorothy was in a class that few men achieve in their lives; it was perfect. Sex is always great in any form if you are a sex addict. I think the only way men can get to perfect is to fantasize about it. I don't think Dot was a sex addict; but any time, any place within reason, any position possible and any amount of time to achieve total satisfaction was the norm.

She would use my body and its erection for her gratification for several minutes, totally concentrating as if I were not there; just a machine with a vibrator attached to it. As if resting, she would then expect me to use her body for my own pleasure. I was only allowed to go so far and she would start again on me as if she could never get enough. This back and forth would go on until we were just too tired to continue.

One of her favorite things to do was to use a small mirror to watch my penis penetrate her, she would watch for a while, lay her head back and usually climax violently. Most men like to watch the same thing but it's easier for us to see it without a mirror.

Dot was always pleasant to be with. She knew I was married and as with all elicit affairs in a foreign country, was aware that I would have to leave someday. I had fleeting thoughts of leaving my wife for her when I retired from the Army but I could not do something like that and living in Greece was not something I would have ever desired.

Every attempt was made by our government to make us as comfortable and happy as possible under the circumstances. Our detachment was over two-hundred air miles and over four-hundred road miles from our headquarters and means of support in Athens. All detachments were directed to have their own bar to keep us from getting drunk in public. While twenty-five percent the country as a whole was considered communist, twenty-five percent of the local population was socialist. Our detachment was very small, about twenty-five or so.

In an attempt to keep our morale up, we could requisition a variety of foods and through the efforts of the cooks we always had an ample supply of steaks, seafood or anything else that everyone would seem to like. The cooks also did an outstanding job of cooking meals off the normal military charts and make meals an art with a variety of dishes only seen in the best buffets. All of our supplies and food were shipped by truck from Athens with stops at two other detachments making us last in the chain.

The truck from Athens was driven by a Greek contractor. He was a friendly man in a jolly sort of way and prone to a good joke, but he always seemed to be late getting to our detachment. The trailer our food was hauled in was insulated and some arrangement was made inside to keep the food cold. I do not recall what that was. A lot of the food was marginal for spoilage and we had to check it real close. After many years from those times, I still have a fear of sour milk or milk that is even close to souring.

We, of course, would over requisition to allow for food that was not fit to eat. We had a lot of freezer and refrigerator space for storage of our rations. We asked the driver on many occasions if he could speed his trips up a little but he would start speaking more in his language than ours claiming, "not to good English." We, of course, knew better.

Then he would say, "It's still food."

There was some sort of payment we had to make to the driver from our slush fund. Probably for some of his trip expenses like food or lodging I believe. This payment was required to be made in drachmas, which is Greek money. Drachmas have been the name for their money for thousands of years and examples of ancient drachmas can be found cheaply all over Greece as souvenirs.

I went to the local town and purchased a small bag of coins that were at least a thousand years old and quite useless. You know what's coming next, don't you? I included those coins as part of his next payment. When confronted, he gave me a perplexed look.

"What's this?" he asked in perfect English.

"It's still drachmas," I answered.

While assigned to base Drama, two American jet fighters shot down two Libyan fighters. The leader of Libya stated he was going to hit American nuclear weapons storage sites in retaliation. We were the only site near the coast. The other two in Greece were too far inland. There were sites in Turkey but no one would dare mess with Turkey. All of our vehicles and the generators we used for power were in the open. I asked our headquarters in Athens for sandbags to at least protect them from small arms fire. Their answer:

"No, we do not want to look concerned."

In January of 1982 I had to return to the state. For the first time, I did not want to leave a lover behind but I had a family so taking her was not even an issue. Dorothy was heartbroken. I did not mean for her to fall in love with me but that's what happen and I considered it my fault.

She was such a nice person. I remember thinking that this is the consequences of my infidelities and I was a first class asshole. Even my recklessness when it came to sex could not justify hurting someone that much.

We spent a last week in Athens while I processed out. At the airport as Dorothy saw me off, she was crying openly. I knew I would never see her again and it hurt. I did not love Dorothy and I never wanted to hurt anyone that bad. On the long flight home, I did some heavy thinking and vowed never to be unfaithful to my marriage again.

I returned to the States and got an administrative job at the replacement detachment at Fort Lewis. This was considered a cushy job and since I was retiring soon, it was appropriate. Serving in Greece left me basically useless to the military anyway. I became a Cold War casualty. A cushy job is what I needed.

.

PART II

LOVE & DEATH

9

Finally, March 1983, I retired from the United States Army. I never belonged in the Army nor did I enjoy my time there. Due to my early training, I was able to perform my duties and excel at them. I was promoted all the way to Sergeant First Class, E-7. My reason for staying in for twenty years was to take advantage of the benefits upon retirement. The medical benefit alone was a big payoff in view of my emphysema later in life.

Thinking back, I should have sought help for what my tour in Greece did to me and stayed in the military. As a senior enlisted man, my duties were much more tolerable and I had a lot to offer. My mind was set on retirement and I lacked proper judgment to know what was best for me.

Within a few days of my retirement, I went to work for a tractor dealership in Yelm, Washington. I was there from day one when they started the company, selling Yanmar tractors and Husqvarna chainsaws. For six months I did not sell one tractor but then all hell broke loose.

I sold fifty units in the next six months. It ended when the owner of the company and his wife did something with all the money from the sales. I never did get all the details but one particular day I arrived at work to find the windows painted out and the other two employees outside with a lost look on their faces.

March 1984, I received word from the man in charge of Yanmar sales in the Northwest of numerous job offers. I would guess it was because of my sales record. I took advantage of a job at Snell Tool Rental in Albany, Oregon and moved there with my second wife and my daughter, Lorrie. I continued selling Yanmar tractors at a blistering pace. I really enjoyed working at Snell Tool as I excelled with hard work.

My wife and I bought a rundown farm house in the outskirts of Lebanon, Oregon. It had several outbuildings which we used as a shop and a chicken house. The one thing that attracted us to the property was a thirty-by-sixty foot building that we could use for raising rabbits. We had gotten into rabbit farming when we lived in Yelm and began to be very good at it. We were one of the few that could make money at it. We were able to get meat rabbits to market in eight weeks while others had to wait ten weeks due to shipping dates and that meant feeding the rabbits two more weeks.

We were lucky enough to go under the wing of sorts of another rabbit grower who had designed a super food that worked. While working with the rabbits, I invented a water system that would not freeze up. Whenever the weather turned cold enough to freeze the water, many lost their system and had to face money-losing repairs. The first system was very complicated and used expensive parts, but it worked very well. After subsequent events and others' attempt to use my invention to their advantage, I re-invented it with off-the-shelf parts and reduced the cost to just a few dollars.

The Breakdown

In October 1986, my wife ruined my life. She decided that she no longer wanted to be with me. She took everything from my life that I ever had and left me a shell. The event blindsided me almost to a state of shock. I did not see it coming. The actual, physical pain in my heart did not leave me for months.

What affected me the most was the cruelty that my wife and her new boyfriend used to implement whatever agendas she had in mind at the time. There were a lot of flirting and long phone conversations that seemed only to antagonize me. She would go to Eugene and spend the day with her new man under the guise of job hunting. At one time she told me that they were going to get a motel room at the Brownsville exit on I-5 so they could just "talk."

Occasionally, we speak of the incident and I believe, purposely, she remembered it all wrong. I believe it was her way of justifying what she did to me. She claimed that she asked me to go away with her to the coast and I kept saying I could not get away from work.

"Excuse me? That's just bull crap."

She became very moody and I kept pursuing her to tell me what was wrong. She said she wanted some time alone with just herself. I told her of course. Later, however, she admitted that she was planning a trip with her male friend. Naturally I was devastated.

From the beginning of this incident, I knew I deserved what was being dished out to me. That did not take the pain away, but it was one of those, "What can I say?" things. I had been such an asshole when it came to infidelity in my marriage. I did not care even if she told me she had slept around while I was overseas those four years in Thailand, Korea and Greece.

My mother told me that when I was on my first tour in Thailand, she and her husband visited my wife and the kids in Tillamook. When they pulled up, they saw a man leave by way of a back window. I was too devastated to care at the time my mother told me the story. I brought it up with her years later and she became very defensive. It still would not bother me; I rather found it kind of hot considering my record of infidelity.

I spent the four months, from October '86 until February '87 trying to convince her to put our marriage back together. Thinking back, what kind of marriage was it? I had volunteered for Viet Nam twice; Korea and Greece, for the good of my military career and to get a break from her. In doing so, I left the kids to her destructive ways and they did not fare well at all. My bad!

I apologized to the kids for my shortcomings as much as I could, but I feel that it did not, nor should not have let me off the hook. I knew soon after we were married in 1964 that it was a mistake. I wanted to walk away from the nuptial numerous times but could not because of the kids. It may sound admirable but it is just basic if you love your children.

Luckily, I am an optimist to the extreme and learned early in my marriage to use the term "yes dear." And again, due to my early training, I stuck in there and made the best of it. I can't say it was all bad. We had a lot of good times exploring, camping, fishing and travelling cross country, visiting many of the states. I would never want anyone to change what or who they are and that holds true with my second wife. I became very good at deflecting her effects on me and my sensitive nature. I don't think the two children we had together survived as well as I did.

I spent three weeks in the mental ward of the VA Hospital in Portland, Oregon. I had a nervous breakdown but was miss-diagnosed as a manic depressive, probably due to my upbeat attitude even in the face of such a destructive relationship.

We held a massive moving sale and sold most of our things with the exception of what we each needed to move on. I was convinced that I would not let her leave me, so in February I loaded my things in an old Ford pickup I had, and moved into my mother's house in Salem, Oregon. My wife let our daughter, Lorrie, move into her boyfriend's parent's house. She moved into one of her boyfriend's apartments and began working with him in whatever endeavors he had going at the time. He never seemed to have a steady job.

On the other hand, I could not work. I had a somewhat uncontrollable shaking that would not go away unless I re-laxed. My mother was a professional artist and was giving painting lessons in her home. She convinced me to start les-sons and like several members of my family, found that I was a natural.

The Reluctant Bachelor

Like any person who experiences being dumped, I was ex-tremely lonely for companionship from the opposite sex. I eventually rented my own apartment and started to live the life of a bachelor. I did not like it but there was no choice, so I decided to try out my new found freedom.

Through personal ads I met a woman with two kids living in Salem. She was nice enough and the sex was great. Her husband had died suddenly and left her with lots of property but no income, so she was living on what she could make in a dead-end job. The property was gone as he had no life insurance to maintain ownership.

We were both lonely for a companion and maybe a more permanent relationship but there was one problem. Her son was about ten and had a discipline problem. He would push his mother to the limit and I did not feel comfortable stepping in, being a newcomer. I think he resented the loss of his father.

She also had a 14-year-old daughter. Truth be told, she was the real problem. When her mother went to work one day, she started playing up to me and letting me know that she was not a virgin and it was ok for me to play house with her. She said she had needs just like her mother. I managed to not be alone with her kids for a day or two and just left.

I probably should have explained myself but I was afraid of repercussions when the daughter tried to explain my accusations so I kept it a secret. I considered that a close-call. Everyone would have taken the 14-year-old's side and I would have been cooked.

Another woman contacted me from the personals. She was living in Lincoln City, Oregon and wanted to meet at a restaurant in Grand Ronde. I was 43 and she was 50 but I did not let the age difference bother me. I could say so much but the three things that best described her was that she was hot, hot, and hot! Thus caused me to wonder why she had no man in her life. The answer took a while.

We talked for a bit and she told me how to get to her apartment near Devils Lake. The next evening I went there and met her son. He was about twelve. She and I chatted for a while and told each other's story. That was pretty much normal, at least that was what I thought at the time. It was getting late so I told her I should be getting back to Salem.

"No, no, you need to tuck me in to bed before you leave."

I may be in a perpetual state of need for sex as any sex addict would be but in order to develop a relationship I didn't think copulating on what was like a first date was a good idea. She got ready for bed and called me into her bedroom. For the first time in my life I tried to pull back from having sex.

She was attractive, smart and seemed to be a normal divorced woman in need of a companion. I did not want to mess up the opportunity to get something going with her. But she made sure that that pull back lasted only a few seconds. She attacked me more or less and would not hear about me leaving. Her son had left with her ex-husband so she wanted to take advantage of the moment. In the ensuing days, the sex was hot, wild and plentiful.

I was in my glory, but it became apparent she had a problem. She could not climax. I am convinced that she was a retired prostitute. She could take a man to places that probably in her past cost a thousand a night and I was getting it free. I could tell she was totally frustrated with herself and I kept trying to please her. I was a bit frustrated with myself also. I really didn't know how to handle the situation. She did not want to talk about it; she just kept trying to climax, trying so hard that it became boring. Yes, that can happen. Boring. All I could do was hang on for the ride.

I kept an apartment in Salem and spent most but not all my time at her place in Lincoln City. It became apparent after a while that it would not work out. I did not want to spend the rest of my life trying to satisfy a frustrated and reformed, alcoholic, nympho ex-prostitute seven years older than me. The way she was working it, she was going to hurt herself physically as she got older.

The one regret I was going to have is that she gave the most amazing blow job I ever had and she enjoyed it immensely. I would not let any woman satisfy me with oral sex unless she really wanted to because she loved it as much as me. She would push me back on the edge of the bed, comfortably get between my legs and take her time. It was obvious that she was enjoying it with passion.

Finders of Lost Love

In August 1987, Jessie came back in my life. My sister was at a five-year class reunion and when Jessie saw her she asked about me.

"He just went through a divorce," my sister informed her.

When she heard that, Jessie likes to say she could not get her phone number out fast enough, as she had herself, just gotten divorced. As they say in the movies, "The rest is history." We had been apart over 25 years. After a phone call, we agreed to meet up in a park in Albany.

I told my girlfriend in Lincoln City that I was going to meet Jessie and honestly informed her who Jessie was. It was innocent at that time; Jessie was a big part of my past. I was anxious to meet her, but did not know what to expect.

My girlfriend went ballistic. It was very ugly. She displayed insane jealousy. I walked out on her and yes, there was a scene. It was inevitable anyway and I could not get out of there fast enough.

It was apparent from the beginning that Jessie and I would begin to socialize together. I didn't know about how she felt but I knew we were going to spend the rest of our lives together. I also know that my extra marital sexual activities were over. Jessie meant everything to me and I vowed that if I had to spend every waking moment of every day for the rest of my life in therapy, I would not stray.

Jessie and I moved on very quickly but decided to wait a year to make any permanent decisions. We wanted to make sure the damage my second wife did to me was not permanent. I was completely over my ex after meeting Jessie again, but I still had that nervous shaking that I had a hard time getting over.

My second wife hates Jessie. It may have stemmed from something Jessie said in Tillamook sometime in 1968 or 1971. It is apparent though that she is very jealous of the relationship between Jessie and me. She makes a fool of herself every time she spits the hate she feels.

Everyone that knows Jessie knows her as a gentle, non-judgmental woman that I would call non-loud rather than quiet. There is no way she deserves the hate projected by my ex. Everyone likes Jessie, especially my children and grandchildren. That alone, makes my ex livid in view of the temperament she has.

Hate is like a wart on your face. You can feel it but you can't see it. On the other hand, everyone else can sees it and will feel it only if you choose to project it. My ex-wife's feelings stand out in that no one accepts her judgment of Jessie.

Jessie and I were married in August 1988 in my mother's backyard. My mother worked very hard to make sure many flowers were blooming that late in the summer for the wedding. As an indication to what kind of person Jessie is, there were many relatives in attendance from her previous marriage! During the ceremony, I became so overwhelmed with emotion that I came close to fainting.

Jessie is such a wonderful person. I get a little choked up just looking at the picture of our wedding day. She is my life and always will be.

We bought a small farm in Albany, Oregon and tried a hand at a u-pick operation. I raised cucumbers and beans mostly. We also had seventy, 40-year-old hazel nut trees. An article was published in the local paper about my prowess at growing green beans.

While the reporters were there they were quite impressed with my tomato crop and the litter of Labrador puppies we had hand raised. The puppy's mother was dead when they were born. We saved ten of the eleven puppies. The vet that cut the puppies from the body of the mother said that was usually not the case. We paid attention to the needs of the puppies and mistakenly fed them lamb's milk replacer at triple strength, which saved their life.

Jessie was laid off from her job at a Smoke Craft so we took advantage of an opportunity to return to Alaska. What an adventure! We soon experienced what we both agreed was the best summer of our lives.

10

I n April 1990, we bought a fourteen foot Lund skiff and a twenty HP motor for our use at the logging camp. The boat would seem to be too small for the job but Lund has an excellent reputation and will float even when full of water and loaded. The camp was located on the ocean, but it was protected by the numerous islands as part of the inside passage that makes up Southeast Alaska.

We drove to Prince Rupert, British Columbia and took the ferry to Ketchikan, Alaska. From there we had to catch another ferry to Prince of Wales Island and drive logging roads to a place called Naukati. From there it was just a few miles in our skiff with Chena, our yellow lab, one of the puppies we raised, and Mindy, our cat, to camp. I was worried about darkness overtaking us and it was a dangerous passage. I had no radio to call camp to tell them we were in Naukati and on the water. I had only made the trip once before when scouting the job weeks before. We made it without incident and arrived with dusk light.

Jessie was the camp cook and housekeeper and I was the bull-cook, carpenter, plumber, electrician and numerous other jobs to include camp fisherman. A lot of our jobs centered on the fact that our boat was the only one that did not leak. The only way into the camp was by boat or plane. That included groceries, mail, visitors and fuel.

For Sunday meals, Jessie would fix cold cuts and we had the day off. We explored the islands in our skiff or went to town, anything to get out of camp. We loved interacting with the wildlife in the area. Eagles were rampant; we could not let our cat outside because of them.

We saw and/or heard numerous whales. In one incident, I was on a scrounge trip in a cove near our camp but could not leave as a whale was feeding in the entrance and I did not want my little skiff butting heads with a multi-ton beast who's brain probably weighed more than I did.

I was charged with building a twenty-by-sixty foot building to house the saws and cutting operations. Heavy rains that Southeast Alaska is known for would have made the operation impossible in the open. A wide door was necessary to accommodate twenty-six foot logs.

Some of these logs were rather large. Our end product required no knots, so these logs were classed as clear. The company we worked for was harvesting spruce on Cap Island. The spruce logs were cut into six by six inches by twenty-six feet cants to be used in all types of musical instruments. These cants were sold to a company in Tacoma, Washington for an exorbitant price, making it worth the time, effort and expense to pursue this type of log in Southeastern Alaska.

In the fall of 1990, we reversed our trip south to visit family. Our plan was to return and winter in the logging camp and start work in the spring. We left our boat and pets in camp of course. After about two weeks in Oregon, we were able to get as far as Craig, Alaska, but due to heavy snow and three feet of water on the logging road, we were told we would not be able to get to the camp for some time.

Wintering in camp was out of the question. Waiting for the roads to clear would have been too expensive as motel prices in Southeast Alaska were extremely high. We returned to Ketchikan and booked passage to Haines, Alaska with the goal of reaching Anchorage.

Meanwhile, Jessie's brother was trying to get our pets, Chena and Mindy, flown to us before we had to leave. Weather forced the float plane carrying them to land and we received a message as we traveled north that he would not make it. He took good care of the animals and two months later, we were able to fly them to Anchorage.

10

After our arrival in Haines, we drove north and spent the night in Tok, Alaska. We did not have a block heater in the pickup we owned at the time and the temperature was twenty-four below zero. Block heaters keep your engines from freezing up and make them easier to start. When they do start the heater having kept the oil warmer, prevents the engine from trying to pump thickened oil. I had to set my alarm for every two hours, get dressed and go outside and start the truck to warm it up. If you want to live in Alaska, you have to adapt and take care of your equipment.

When we got to Anchorage, we stayed in a long term place called the Sourdough Motel on Government Hill. Within days, I was hired as a carrier with the Anchorage Times newspaper. Jessie also got a job with a temp agency and went to work at the Anchorage Veterans Affairs Office. A year later, Jessie was hired as a full time employee and went on to work for them over twenty-three years.

In the spring of 1991, we moved out of the Sourdough Motel having rented half a duplex on Newt Drive. My job with the Anchorage Times turned into an adventure. I worked my way up to area south manager, and in December of 1991, I became an independent contractor responsible for eastern Alaska. This meant leaving Anchorage in the middle of the night and driving over 500 miles every day!

On one particular night when we left Anchorage, the temperature was about thirty-eight and it was drizzling. When we got to the end of the route in Copper Center, it was fifty below zero. When we got back to Anchorage, it was raining and near forty. Those kinds of temperatures are really hard on the vehicles and the drivers.

Jessie's son would drive relief some nights and two or three nights a week we would take two vehicles. Eventually, I had to drive to Tok two to three times a week to collect money. I hired two other people in Glennallen. One drove to Tok seven days a week from Glennallen after I dropped his papers off. One of the vehicles we used more often because of the gas mileage. I had to change the oil every eight days.

My immediate supervisor for the Glennallen route was a 30-something-year-old wise ass. The newspaper business is all about the number of subscribers and I guess he thought driving sixteen hours a day and 500 or more miles a night just wasn't enough effort to make him look good.

He asked me in front of several area managers for a five percent increase in home delivery and business subscribers. Unbeknownst to him, I had hired the two helpers in Glennallen and had about 200 new starts in my bags. Again in front of several of his coworker, I peeled off about 30 starts and handed them to him.

"Is that all you want?" I asked.

Then, I told him not to push me or he could get someone else to take the run. Everyone knew only a crazy man would take the job. His supervisor came out of her office.

"Hey, leave him alone or I'll send you out as his relief," she quipped.

In early May of '92, I was in Tok on business for the Anchorage Times. One of my customers was a popular restaurant and they were very busy. The parking lot was full of RVs and it was apparent tourists were trying to get a jump on Alaska's short seasons. Tok is the first town in Alaska after a rather long and hard road from Haines Junction in Canada. It was mid-morning. Wet and slick snow was blowing sideways. It was plastered all over the sides of buildings, cars, trucks and their RVs.

I could sense these people were thinking, "Is this what I just drove several thousand miles for?" They were staring out of the windows and talking in muffled tones. I felt a little sorry for them, but that didn't stop me from wanting to have a little fun at their expense.

"How about this weather?" the waitress, speaking loudly asked.

The room went silent as ears strained to hear an explanation of what they considered impossible for the month of May.

"Well," I sighed, "it's pretty mild for such an early spring. It's like this all the way to Anchorage." I added, "Sticking real good too."

I passed out several free newspapers and left, leaving the waitress to explain.

"He was only kidding, really."

Eventually, the stress of sixteen-hour drives of 500-plus miles took a toll on me and the vehicles. On one occasion, I was talking with a co-worker and in mid-sentence and I fainted. My legs just went out from under me. The supervisor and of course myself, thought it not a good idea for me to drive without some extra rest. I called Jessie. She and her son had to drive that night. Because of insurance, Jessie's son could only drive one of our vehicles.

On another stroke of bad luck, in a heavy wet snow downfall, I ran over a rockslide and pushed the oil pan into one of the crankshaft ends. I limped into King Mountain Lodge and phoned Jessie again about 2am. They had to bring another vehicle and I drove the damaged one home and to the dealer the next day for repairs. Then the unexpected happened: the sale of the paper and my loss of a job. We had driven our three vehicles a total of over 86,000 miles in five months!

Before I went to work for the Anchorage Times, it had been sold by the family that started the paper over 50 years before. There had been two papers in Anchorage for decades. The man who bought the Times decided to take on the other paper. He almost gave papers away and was rumored he was losing almost a million dollars a month.

I was given up to 1400 papers a month but only delivered or sold less than half of them. They told me to dispose of the ones I did not sell, so I hauled them back to the paper and let them worry about it. I did not want to play that game.

Again, it was all about numbers. Additionally, they let me keep any monies that I collected from subscribers and the single copy boxes outside businesses. We assumed that when the Times drove the other paper out of business that they would raise the price of the paper in outlining areas and change their business tactics to start making money. In the end, they were losing money with my route and charging Anchorage prices for the paper.

In early spring of 1992, I went to the paper for draw changes. I was told that the paper had been sold to the competitor and that night was to be my last run. What a shock. As hard as the route was, I considered this good news. Reality had not set in yet.

Others at the paper were given thirty minute notice to clear out their desks and leave the building. In subsequent months, over two dozen people working for the paper were forced into bankruptcy. We held out for a year but could not avoid it.

11

EMPHYSEMA

If you have ever had to listen to someone expound on their illnesses, injuries or the numerous pills they are taking, then you know that no one cares. You can fake interest but we all know most of us do not have the courage to tell them, "Hey, I'm not interested."

I must tell my story in hopes that I can stop someone from smoking. Hopefully, someone in my own family or many others, will not start or maybe even better, entice smokers to quit.

This disease started in December 1992. My emphysema came on suddenly. I caught a bad cold but it was different this time. I would get very dizzy whenever I bent over and I could not breathe very well. I had never had these things happen to me before so I knew something was wrong. Being a smoker for so long, I kind of sensed what it was.

You tell yourself for years that when you get sick then you will quit smoking. But when you get sick, emphysema has been with you for a long time and it is too late. When the symptoms struck me, I was four months and forty-nine years young.

I made an appointment with family practice on Elmendorf Air Force Base as I was eligible for retired military medical benefits. The doctor I saw was very distracted with the doctor in the next room. They were planning a trip on their snow machines that weekend. I told the doctor that I had a bad cold and could not breathe. I also told him that I was coughing up blood, was dizzy most of the time and my ears were ringing. He arranged an appointment with ENT (Ear, Nose and Throat).

"Good. Maybe they will get to the bottom of this," I thought.

The ENT doctor gave me a hearing test and told me he had bad news: I needed a hearing aid. That's when I lost it. I told him all of my symptoms and that my ears were the least of my problems. He scheduled an appointment with the right doctor and my health records promptly disappeared. They did not want others to see their sloppy dealings with a serious condition.

My first "real" doctor gave me instructions on how to use the inhalers and other meds that I would be taking for the rest of my life. He ordered oxygen equipment and a local supplier helped me learn how to use it. After treating me for two years, the doctor called me at home to tell me he was leaving Alaska and to wish me luck.

He told me, "I didn't think you would live this long."

Every doctor for the subsequent years told me almost the same thing.

They would say, "You're a very sick man, Mr. Jennings."

I never did believe any of them and I think that's what kept me going so long.

Into the Smoke

Regardless of what I may have wanted, I must admit that my stepfather influenced me. When I was younger, I vowed never to be like him. The Army changed all that. I went into the Army in August of 1960, choosing not to finish high school. My stepfather was killed in the spring of that year and I felt free and a need to explore the world. Additionally, I felt my mother did not need another mouth to feed besides my two sisters.

From the $80 plus I earned per month I thought I could send some money home. However, weak willpower for spending kept that from happening. The most important reason for leaving school was I was told by my counselor that I would not have enough credits to graduate with my classmates. I had an IQ of 130 and was sure school was a waste of time anyway. When I raised my right hand to take the enlistment oath I was just fourteen days and seventeen-years-old.

The US Army of those days used a daily training schedule to tell soldiers what to do and when to do it. Incorporated in some of our daily activities was a smoke break. An example would be a training class and a break would be scheduled as part of the class. Smoking was an approved activity in society also. We would leave the class and mill around a cigarette butt. Those who had cigarettes would have to share.

"Can I bum a smoke?"

I would be asked hundreds of times a day, or so it seemed that often.

The training I received from my stepfather was, "When told to jump, you hit the ceiling and at full dive speed and gladly do what you have been told." I soon learned to carry cigarettes to please those around me.

Years later when I graduated from counseling, I found that my stepfather had instilled in me the undying need to please those around me even if it meant giving up everything I owned. Now, where did I get those cigarettes?

The 60's Army would rotate there stock of C or K rations by serving them in the mess hall. These were field rations meant for combat troops and some of them were dated from the 40's. They would have a server at the end of the chow line standing in front of a large container of cigarette packs—five or twenty cigarettes—insisting that you take them even if you didn't smoke.

"Give them to your buddies," he would say.

That was right up my alley.

I seemed to recall that it was February of 1961 that I smoked my first cigarette. It was on the back entrance steps of the 4th Aviation Company barracks on Fort Lewis, Washington. It was from a fresh pack of Pall Mall's red pack I had bought from the Post Exchange.

"Wow, did that taste good!" I recall.

I was hooked for over twenty-seven years. I even quit for five years between 1973 until 1978. A year in Korea mixed with lots of booze and inhaling the seducing smoke in the NCO club helped me get started again.

During the years 1993-96, I seemed to tolerate emphysema very well. Maybe it was due to my relatively young age, my overall lung capacity and my tendency to ignore the fact that I was sick.

I went to work in an art gallery in downtown Anchorage and my good friend, and a great Alaskan artist, Diane Drashner, taught me mat cutting. I started my own mat cutting and picture framing business and soon had more work than I could handle. I spent most of my time cutting mats for others to resale. I supplied Anchorage Saturday Market booths, craft fairs, art galleries, and even booths at the Alaska State Fair. All of my work was sold before it was started. As a business person, that would be great but I am an artist and the repeating the same cuts for hours a day became very tedious.

In early fall of 1996, I drove South and brought my son, Greg, and his three children to Alaska. Greg's wife had run off and left the kids with him. Greg is a carpenter and went to work in Anchorage and I concentrated on taking care of my grandkids.

I sold my cutting equipment to a customer but kept the company name and my cut patterns. All of us moved into a large four bedroom house in Chugiak, just north of Anchorage. When Greg took his wife back, Jessie and I went through the process of buying and getting a house built in Wasilla. Our house was built on West Balboa Drive in Wasilla. We moved into it in October 1997.

In the summer of 2001, my son, Gene, his wife and my grandson, came to Alaska for a visit. We had reservations at Denali Park for the motor home. While traveling there, my grandson had seen several lakes, most of which were long and slender. We were passing Summit Lake in Broad Pass on the Parks Highway. The lake is over two and a half miles long and just four-tenths of a mile wide. I was driving and my grandson was in the passenger seat.

He asked, "Grandpa, why are all of the lakes up here so long and skinny?"

"So we can fit the fish in them," I replied.

He was silent for a moment and then said, "That many, huh?"

"No," I said, "that big."

On the way back home from this trip I ran out of oxygen and could not breathe. I was laying on the couch in the motor home and Gene was driving. I was crying and Jessie was trying to comfort me. Gene stopped at a remote restaurant at Mile 135 of the Parks Highway to call for help. The staff asked what the matter was and when told, they said that they had a bottle of medical oxygen that we could have. It had been there for years. It was full and meant we did not have to call for medical assistance.

An ambulance that far from town would have cost a small fortune and a helicopter would have cost ten times as much. When we got home, I went to the hospital for treatment of another pulmonary exasperation. Weeks later, I was telling a good friend of the incident. He let me finish my story and then told me that he and the Mayor of Nenana, Alaska had left that very oxygen bottle there on the way to Fairbanks five years earlier. A small world I would guess.

In May 2002, we brought my daughter, Lorrie, to Alaska. She lived with us for about nine years. In February of 2003, we moved into our house on South St. John Court. It was the same floor plan as our house on Balboa but with a second floor. This gave us twice the room and gave Lorrie her own apartment.

During the years of 2004-2010, I had numerous pulmonary exasperations and emergency room visits, too many to count. My eyes began to fail and I had to have double cataract replacement. I had internal bleeding after a routine procedure and heavy loss of blood when they tried to fix it. Blood loss caused mild brain damage indicated by short term memory loss. Once, I drove the Alcan in two days and hardly remembered the trip.

Jessie has had a knee replacement, an ankle fusion and spinal surgery. Old age is taking its toll; however, she looks like she is still in her 50's. She is working and commuting almost sixty hours a week, well respected and liked at her job. She wants to retire but I think she is too valuable to the Veterans Administration. I call her the "Little Wig" of the VA. I advised her to wait until I died to retire.

In 2011 we discovered that Jessie's brother, Gary, had been living in an abusive situation perpetrated by an elderly couple that he had been working for, and living with, for twenty-four years. These were the people who owned the logging company we worked for in 1990. With the help of several local people in the isolated area where they lived, we managed to get her brother on a plane and brought him to Wasilla. As Lorrie has returned to Oregon, he moved into her apartment.

Gary was a huge help to me around the house and yard, as I was slowly becoming useless. I was to the point that I can do nothing but get in the way. I do manage to cook all of the meals and pay the bills.

By 2012, my emphysema has been acting up and I was not doing well. This has been going on since about January with a slow lead up to a pulmonary exacerbation. Sometime in March, I went to bed late, around 10pm and knew when I laid back on the pillow that I was in trouble for sure. I woke Jessie up. Without moving much, which consumed too much oxygen, I told her I had to go to the Emergency Room.

Jessie began to get me dressed and up. I believe Gary was there for that also. They got me to the truck by walking me just a few feet at a time. Breathing was hard for me as it is with all exacerbations. We spent most of the night in the ER.

It seemed a little harder than usual to get my lungs to bring the oxygen levels up and keep them there. I do not remember them X-raying my lungs during the emergency room visit. Normally, I bounce back fast but this time I think I should have listened to the doctor and let him keep me for observation. Since I have a lot of support at home I talked my way out of the hospital.

The bad times continued for three months. I could not walk twenty feet without slowing or resting. Stairs were so hard I had to stop and lean on something to get my breath back. I could do very little for myself without running out of oxygen. I survived by taking massive doses of steroids and antibiotics.

The Suicidal Spirit

Thoughts of what others call suicide were rampant with me. If you have to pee, you pee. If you are sleepy, you sleep. If you are hungry, you eat. However, if you suffer as I was, you look for a way to end it. It just came naturally with me. It no longer bothered me to leave this earth. Any zest for life is overridden by a need for death. I was tolerating my current conditions and I knew that if one more serious event came along that without hesitation, I would end it.

Every time I would go to the emergency room or to a routine appointment, they would ask if I had thoughts of suicide or thoughts of hurting myself. This is part of the screening process.

"Well, hell yeah!"

At least that is what I really wanted to say. But if you tell them, then you're not serious. If you say, "Yes, I want to kill myself," then you're just looking for sympathy or attention.

I would just smile to myself when they ask and say no. Their queries were so juvenile, what did they expect me to say? I did want to go to Oregon one more time to see my family.

It was during this period when I was so sick that I became aware of a presence. During those first six months of 2012 and always without prior thought, an image of my mother would flash into my mind. She was always smiling and usually sitting on her couch at her home in Salem, Oregon where she lived for over forty years.

She always would come when I was least expecting her. I would be preparing dinner, showering, or engrossed in a TV program; anything but thinking about her. The image only lasted a fraction of a second. Although never unpleasant, they were always strong and very intrusive.

During those months of suicidal ideations, she was with me often and her presence was strengthened by her eventual absence. When my upcoming adventure was over and I was back in Alaska, she stopped appearing. Never without a purpose, would she leave me with the knowledge that it was just not my time to die.

Sometimes I think of death and dying and I welcome it. It does not keep me from being apprehensive about the moment I finally cross over. What helps me get past what I think those last moments will be, is those things that happen while I was in the hospital. The happenings were real and whenever I feel like doubting, I let reassurance come over me. This is my religion.

Any spiritual person can relate to these feelings because they are the same relationship they have with God. I just do not believe as they do, but I know why they need their crutch. So, basically you can say reassurance is my religion.

My primary doctor is an internal medicine specialist and she had referred me to a pulmonary specialist in Anchorage. He had removed prescribed medications from my list and tried a few new ones with mixed results. Like so, the emergency room doctor had removed me from even more medications and I thought I was almost bare of bronchodilators.

For two months, my breathing became worse. I had to begin using my electric scooter for any necessary trips and curtail any get-out-of-the-house trips. Gary had to go with me for anything I wanted to do.

I had been planning a trip to Albany, Oregon to see my grandkids, son and daughter and their families. I assumed that my condition was permanent and that this would be my last trip down the road. I would not be dissuaded; I was going.

I loaded up the motor home and had Jessie's brother, Gary, to accompany me, for there was no way I could do much of anything but drive. He was a huge help and I could not have made the trip without him.

My motor home had two oxygen concentrators, one being the backup, powered by an AC inverter and numerous tanks of oxygen in the event the system gave out. As luck would have it, it did. After staying overnight in a RV Camp in Houston BC, the inverter alarm went off because the voltage dropped below ten. I went on tanks.

Just before getting to Prince George, BC, I stopped for gas and discovered that I could just barely get out of the driver's seat. Faintly, I could hear the hiss of the freeway traffic but it was fading in and out, more of a throbbing noise. I believe now that my lung was about to collapse and whoever was assigned to be my guardian angel was totally vigilant.

We stopped in Quesnel, BC at a RV repair shop. The mechanic said the converter would not charge the batteries and had to be replaced. He suggested I get it in the states because it was about $600 in Canada. I drove across the border early so as to get through the Seattle traffic and stayed in a rest area. I was in a hurry to get this motor home fixed because I prefer the concentrators rather than tanks.

I arrived in Albany on the 23rd of June and settled in the Blue Ox RV Park. After hooking the motor home up to the RV park electricity, I called a mobile RV repair service and they determined that the two RV batteries were bad—frozen during the last winter.

12

DEATH?

S ometime in the very early hours of June 26th I got out of bed and went to the bathroom to pee. I do not remember feeling anything of what was to come, getting up and walking six to eight feet in the motor home seemed normal. As I left the bathroom though, I realized that I could not breathe. There must have been enough oxygen in my system to get me up. Outside the bathroom, I discovered that I could not move.

I leaned on the back of the dinning bench for over fifteen minutes, frozen in place. I was taking short breaths and could not get any air into my lungs. Moving like a snail, I got to my cell phone and started calling my son and daughter, Gene and Lorrie. It was three or 4am that I eventually got them on their way. I knew I was having some kind of major event.

Thinking back, I was not thinking right at all. I should have called 911. I believe I thought I could have fixed whatever was wrong. My kids said I was very lucky because they had their phones turned down. Regardless, it seemed to me it took forever for someone to get to my motor home. Someone help me with a nebulizer breathing treatment but it did not work. I then had Lorrie call 911 for help.

I only remember parts and short moments of the next few days and what I do remember is not in order. After the ambulance and I arrival at the ER, the doctor ordered an X-ray and told me my right lung was not functioning. It had collapsed. Bottom line: when you have emphysema, it's serious.

My son and daughter watched as the emergency room doctor, using a scalpel, cut a hole in the upper right part of my chest. He inserted a tube between my ribs and my lung to re-inflate the lung. Lorrie said I was in a sitting position when they did this and I remember that it hurt—a lot. I do believe shortly after feeling the doctor cut into me with his scalpel that I went into shock. I don't remember much of the next few hours.

On day two in the hospital, they had managed to restored my lung and place me in a room for observation. They had a vacuum devise hooked to my lung to help it stick to the chamber wall. They attempted to seal the hole in my chest around the tubing with a lot of tape. One of the medical personnel told me it was ok to cough. I did and all hell broke loose.

A lot of air went under my skin. Most of my upper body was swollen so much that I could not do anything but stare at the ceiling through squinted eyes. My neck was swollen too much to look down. Air under the skin spread to all parts of my chest, back, arms and even the top of my head.

I remember all of the doctors and nurses thought I was having an allergic reaction to something and gave me two atropine injections. Another doctor entered the room and told them I had a condition called *subcutaneous emphysema*. Another name was *Crepitus*. It was with me for weeks. People would come by my room in weeks to come to feel and see the effects of this condition as most did not get a chance to see it in their medical training.

Later, one thing that was very clear to me while lying flat on my back, I recalled what the ER doctor said.

"Mr. Jennings, I don't know what else to do for you. I don't know how to get you out of this hospital."

For some strange reason, what he said did not bother me. This may have taken place on day three. My mother began flashing her appearance. It was very strong and often. I became aware that what was happening was an un-programmed event, an accident out of the time line of my life.

All of the events that were taking place where not to be. I had a strong feeling that no matter what may happen, just get through it and everything would be all right—I am sure, that is what my mother was telling me. It worked. I remained cheerful and did not worry in the least about what doom and gloom everyone seemed to pass my way. It's very strange: I worried more about that thing they shoved up my penis than the possibility of a snip job and a huge shot of morphine so I could pass over.

Gene and Lorrie took my motor home out of the RV Park and returned my rental car. The next day, one of the doctors told them they had better call friends and family in as I may not make it past Monday.

A local pulmonologist came forward with a procedure, a clinical trial program not yet totally approved in the U.S. Since I was basically going to die, Albany General Hospital was accredited to do the operation because I was there and not going anywhere.

While the doctor explained what was wrong with me and what they were offering, Jessie took careful notes. What they were to do to me was called a mercy operation. I was dying so anything was ok with me but I don't remember. I'm glad Jessie made the right decision to proceed with their recommendations. I can always feel her pain whenever I perused her notes.

No one knew if the procedure would be a success or what my chances would be. I was the oldest of the 300 in the United States to get this operation. The procedure has been performed for many years in other countries. I guess they were trying to see how to make money in our country before they gave its approval.

The lung reduction surgery that this procedure replaced was not too successful and I was advised for years to turn down reduction surgery. Many died from the operation or spent the rest of their lives in recovery.

Small devices would be installed in my lung to plug air leaks. These devices resemble tiny parachutes with a series of hooks at one end. The research for this procedure meant the devices were constantly being upgraded or improved. The latest were hand carried from San Diego by the engineer that created them. She was met at the airport and was allowed to help place them in my lung. Operating on emphysema patients is very precarious and many doctors had told me I would not survive.

A second operation had to be done. Whether it was my strong will to live or my guardian angel, either way, I lived. I like to think it was a combination of all things, including the skill of the doctor and the caring atmosphere of all the people at Samaritan Albany General Hospital.

I was in ICU for two weeks. Because of the unusual nature of the procedure and many complications that I had, again I was the center of attention for most of the two weeks. The recovery of my lung function surpassed all of the doctor's expectations.

In one incident, my son Gene and I were joking around about the past and we went into a laughing fit. I began to swell up again as air was forced under my skin from the strong laughter spasms. This was very serious; however, I didn't become overly concerned. Gene said it just happened before his eyes and soon I could not bend my neck and could only see the ceiling. We just kept it down a little.

The swelling went down in a few days but it gave everyone on the medical staff a scare. The way I had to get the air from under my skin was to work the swelling from my belt line, chest and head up to my neck with my hands and out of my tear ducts. From then on everyone joked about not making me laugh or I would laugh myself to death.

One strange thing: a few days after the operations I noticed a reemergence of my creativity. I was able to think ahead and put sentences together like I did in my 30's. I no longer seemed to depend on spell check as much. I have never been able to do that. For years I would have to stutter around what I was trying to say until I remembered the words. Now, they just came out as fast as I could think.

Thoughts were coming out of my brain so fast I began to take notes in case I forgot them. I will keep that notebook forever. I have never been verbally articulate enough to put two sentences together, much less the contents of this book. This ability came to me a few days into my stay in the ICU and it has not left since. I equate this to people who awake from a coma speaking a foreign language they never spoke before.

While waiting permission from the doctor to travel again, I decided to publish my cookbook that I had been working on for about a year. I made fifty copies on CDs and after buying a cheap printer, I made twenty-five copies in binders. I shared these copies with many people at the hospital.

In July, gaining travel permission, we loaded up the motor home and Gene and I headed home to Alaska. The trip took four days and it was a nightmare for me. I was in severe pain and had to stay on powerful pain pills for the duration of the drive. Gene did almost all of the driving and I strapped myself to the couch to lay down. Many would enjoy the pills they made me take but I did not. Sure, they numb the pain but I vowed not to get hooked on these drugs.

13

BACK TO THE FUTURE

L ife is like assholes: everyone has one, and we can't avoid acknowledging its existence. Some like to keep theirs quiet and some just let it rip. The latter is where we get so much "stinkin' thinkin'."

If I had to live my life over again, what would I change? I tell others not a thing. One of my life's lessons is that I learned a lot at the time and had fun doing it. But, I hurt a lot of people and they don't even know it.

I realize I was lucky to get all my bad activity out of my system before Jessie came back into my life. I would like to say that that was why I was so bad early on, but that is not true. My early life must have formed my later attitudes and actions in all matters.

I lacked the education, knowledge, fortitude or maturity to get past the ability to commit all those hurtful indiscretions. Having never known or remembering my real father, nor having anything to do with him, I wonder, maybe I was just like him. I will not use that as an excuse.

In my story, I often referred of myself as a sexual addict. I certainly show symptoms of that condition, but I believe I may be using it as a crutch or justification or for a better word, an excuse. I think there is no getting past the fact that I had no self-control.

I probably am just like my real father and my stepfather. Having no self-control may have been inherited or learned, I don't know. I had the intelligence to get past it but choose not to. I have known a lot of men just like me and ironically, I did not like them. Yes, I admit this is hypocritical; just another on my long list of faults.

I would like it to be known that I have not written this story, my memoirs, to justify or apologize for my actions; let's call it an exposure. Mankind's future will bring forward knowledge of inherited and learned traits, so let's call my story a warning. For some reason, I find that amusing.

Like every living human, I cannot take the past back, nor can I apologize enough. Honestly, as I stated previously, I would not change it. I also do not want to spend the rest of my short time left trying to explain or justify myself. Admission to my actions and faults does not give me relief from responsibility. I also do not want to waste time blaming others. So, the only recourse is to get on with life from here and look at the past experiences like perpetual dung in the barnyard of life, meant to disappear and spring life anew in the new harvest.

There isn't time for any verbal or emotional deception.

I have set my life's lessons, force and experiences adrift without an anchor or a string to pull it back.

The rudder can steer or flap loosely in the currents that remain.
It no longer matters where it has been or where it's going.
We should not care, only experience the good of the final voyage
and if calm seas are not found, ignore those who would cause strife.
I shall die with peace.

14

LIFE ANEW?

In 2013, I started writing about things in the present and as they unfold. Perhaps I will add to my story until the book is printed and then I will not have a choice but to quit writing. I am still very close to death and maybe the process will be interesting. This chapter will contain some of my current thoughts and I think I will leave them in even as some will become irrelevant as life changes. I can do that. It's my book.

Even though it was not my time after all, I came close to death. I keep fooling myself into believing that it does not bother me. Given the ability to express myself in writing while in the hospital and realizing that I am impressed with life, I guess I better start writing some of life's events. This writing is not a bestseller; rather it is something to leave to my family in addition to my paintings. I challenge present and future members of my family to add to my story; let's keep it an ongoing thing lest we be forgotten.

Can you imagine reading the life events of my ancestors in the Mormon movement as they traveled west? Or can you imagine my grandmother's story of the escape from the Mexican rebels as they ran from the Mormon settlements in Mexico? Members of her party had to burn a railroad bridge to stop their pursuers or none of us would be here. Do a web search for "Mormon settlements in Mexico" for a complete story. I must pass these stories down, second hand from my mother. It would be great if I could read them written in her words.

They say to make a stone sculptor, just knock off the parts that don't belong to what you are trying to sculpt and you are finished. An artist knows it's never good enough and a painting is never finished, but with a life story, the facts are there. Just knock off the bull-crap and get it out there.

Tell the truth or it's never finished. Be prepared though: you cannot explain the facts of your life with "it's hard to explain" or "it's complicated." You're going to piss off a few but if they can't take the truth, they shouldn't read your story. Then again, be objective. Their truth may be better than yours.

In March 2013, I traveled from Alaska to Oregon to pick up my daughter. She wished to come back to Alaska. I had told her when she left that she never really leaves Alaska and I guess she got hooked again. I would never tell her but my main reason for going back to Oregon was to see the doctor that saved my life.

As crazy as it may sound—even for a man preparing for his own demise—I am weak when it comes to the loss of life, particularly with domesticated animals. For example, when my daughter's dog, Murphy, died, I was very shook up. The pain of loss was too great and to me, it cannot make up for the joy pets bring over the years. I have been this way for as long as I can remember. Jessie and I refuse to get another pet. To me, it is like losing a child every ten or twelve years.

I made a follow up appointment before I left Alaska. I believe the doctor was genuinely glad to see me. I was his

first patient for the procedure that saved my life and the out-
come—though doubtful at the time—turned out exception-
ally well. Many of the people who were involved in my care
were there that day and they were quite busy telling the new
people around us about the events in June 2012 that changed
my life. They called me their miracle man. These were very
touching moments.

My plan for winter 2013 was to stay in Oregon for at least
five months. It will be a trial of escaping the winter air in my
house in Wasilla. The plan failed. I became very weak and
had to turn back in Watson Lake, BC.

Over the years, I presume I have traveled the Alcan Highway
over eighty times. I have lost count of how many times I have
driven the Alcan. Each time I forget, I round down to the last
number I can remember and start from there. I am sure I
have driven that road many times past eighty. I have become
numb to each trip that I make. I start off with the enthusiasm
of a well-rested body and when I was younger, I would push
through without regard to eating or resting.

After a day or two of that, it becomes apparent that this
trip is not as short as you thought so I would take a break.
Now, the first night's rest is as important as the last and it
takes me four days to take a trip that I have taken in as little
as two days. The two day trip was a nightmare of stupidity. I
have calculated that I have spent almost a year of my life driving the Alcan Highway from Alaska to Oregon.

As old age sets in, I can remember every mile of the trip.
But sometimes as my insecurity sets in as well, I have to count
the tunnels in the Frasier Canyon again to make sure there
are still seven of them.

There are places along the Alcan where I can see old sections that I had driven in the 60's, mingling and sharing space with the places that I had enjoyed observing in the 70's, all ingredients in today's modern pavement: a hard surfaced, high speed road that is several miles shorter than it was when it was built.

It is the 26th of June, 2013. It has been one year since the event. I sense I cannot make it much longer. I have chest pains almost daily and it is almost impossible to keep my heart rate below 100. Several times in the last month I think my system has tried to shut down but I forced a breath and came back.

I still have jobs to do. I have to get the house in Houston (Alaska) finished. I have paintings to finish, even though I have experienced a painters block for years. I have to get Jessie's finances in order.

And now, two months later, I am as good as I can be in my 21st year with emphysema. It is all a matter of taking the right medicine and taking it correctly. The details are not as important as the results. A new and common medicine has given me a lot of energy to add to my ever-present drive.

Overall, my system is shutting down. I feel good when at rest and can breathe well as long as I do not move. I can tell that there is no going back from this; no magic pill to fix this. A doctor in my primary care clinic has referred me to an end-of-life case manager.

The day after he talked to me, I became very depressed. Probably the worse I have ever experienced but I got through it. He also wanted to prescribe powerful anti-depressants, adding that I was going to enter a panic state. Knowing that I now had over 200 pain pills, when I can't breathe while sitting at rest, I will end it by just going to sleep.

The winter of 2013-2014 has been a low snow year. No snow cover and the glacier and volcanic dust that is so common to the south central part of the state is raising havoc on my system. I now realize that I will have to leave Alaska, at least for half of the year.

Memories of my past are becoming so vivid and clear that I almost believe I am there. I am recalling things I thought I had forgotten years ago. I now realize the memories were always, not forgotten, but dormant and just waiting to be stroked and caressed in the torment we live before death.

Some say that just before an accident that our whole life flashes before us. That may be true but when you are dying the slow death of emphysema, the flash can take decades. I believe that's what's happening to me. Most of my memories would bore anyone else but me. They are mine alone and if I can learn from them, so be it. If they can teach someone else, then that is great. If they are humorous, using my best attempt at humor, I would try to make others laugh at my expense.

On the other hand, ingrained in the vivid memories are some things that are so insignificant, I wonder why they are there: colors, texture, weather, smells, and feelings. Where do these things come from?

My trip to Oregon is delayed until early spring. I cannot travel alone as I cannot walk more than a few feet nor carry anything.

Late December 2013, my mother once again began flashing me. She has appeared several times and again, as before, none of the times was she on my mind. My medical condition is as bad as it can be without being sick in some way. I am ready for anything but I just don't want pain. I have a high tolerance for pain but I feel I have to be apprehensive about something.

I barely made it into 2014. Upon the arrival of the new year, I have had a really bad pulmonary event. It's getting very hard to weather these spells. Moving is near impossible. Again, it's the dust levels in the air with a snowless winter. My primary doctor told Jessie and I that I am one pneumonia away from death. A bad cold will do it.

I made my trip to Oregon in early spring and my condition got much better. Soon after returning to Alaska, I became much worse and moving even ten feet is difficult. My doctor wanted me to enter the care of hospice but after the initial interview I was told they could not qualify me for funding. I believe that my upbeat and always positive attitude misled the interviewer. I was finally convinced to start taking opiates and was told they would help my breathing. I believed my doctors. After a few months my body became addicted to Percocet and if it helps my lungs to function better, who cares?

Mid-year June 2014 was the two-year anniversary of my lung collapse. Most of the time just moving can make me feel faint. My body systems have adapted to low oxygen so well that oxygen levels of seventy-four are common. Recently, my oximeter registered sixty-three and I spent fifteen minutes trying to recover from seventy-four. Jessie was helping me lay on the bed and I was sure my time had come. However, I recovered but I feel time slipping away. Soon, moving will be impossible and I will have to end it. I can't say that does not bother me but as I said before, I have one more painting to do. I have decided that it will be my best.

One of my doctors recently told me that people with my condition drown. He said they do an autopsy and find too much fluid in their lungs for them to function. This explains why in late stages of emphysema, we become very good at coughing up the "crap" caused by the irritants like dust, smoke and mold that we breathe in. Finally, we just can't keep up.

It is like walking into water that is getting progressively deeper and deeper. We eventually have to bounce to the surface to breath and when it gets too deep or we get too tired, we give up and drown. When I am laying or sitting still, I am fine, but when I move, even across the room, my system will not keep up. The water is getting too deep and I am about to experience that last bounce. What would you do?

Redemption, I mentioned earlier taking the medicine correctly is essential. My inhalers have a dose counter built in. I glance at it once or twice a week and if there is a number there, I assume I am ok. My old eyes can't see the small number used so I don't try. I pumped it twice, suspecting malfunction and it did not work. I realized I didn't remember the last time I opened a new inhaler but it had been three or four months. I have not had any of my primary medicine for that period and that explains why I am doing so badly. After one week back on the inhaler, I am feeling much better. I was close to taking an overdose of Percocet to end the misery. It was that bad.

Before I die, I must confess that staying faithful to Jessie has not been a problem. Someone that important in a person's life is a sure cure for any uncontrollable wandering that I suffered from as love conquers and overrides all. My second wife was in no way responsible for my wandering ways, nor did she contribute to my desire to be as bad as I was. It just happened and I kept it from her.

It's August of 2014. I had a long conversation with my second wife. She is the one that unknowingly took the brunt of my many years of indiscretions. We discussed this story but not in detail. I advised her not to read it and she agrees. I hope she does not; I would never want to appear to have written this as a form of revenge.

It was apparent to me that she was the one I most wanted to tell of the existence of this story. Jessie is aware of it as I stated before and had encouraged me to do what I wanted to do. It is hard to get Jessie to express her true opinion. She understands that there is a darker version of my life during the twenty-five years that we were separated.

After writing this story, I can see the many times that I should have sought help. I was so use to keeping secrets that I must have been afraid of exposure. Again, I would avoid any discussion of my sex life, I think because of my early trauma. Right or wrong, it's over.

The only person in my story to get a good dose of inflicted revenge is me. Modern medicine keeps coming up with new procedures or drugs to keep me alive. The latest started August 2014 and I am breathing extremely well. So, they fill me with drugs to help me breathe better and narcotics to keep me from feeling sorry for myself.

Perhaps I should have written my story, left it on my computer and checked out. Give credit to the will to live. There have been about 107 billion deaths of modern man on this earth and the fear of death has had a long time to ingrain itself in our makeup.

Hospice

At the end of September 2014, those around me, both family and medical professionals, have convinced me to finally go into hospice. Unlike before, I think they were right. While resting, my oxygen levels are fine but any movement to accomplish normal tasks on my part causes my oxygen levels to drop into a very dangerous areas. I believe it is great that my body has adapted to low oxygen levels, but it is apparent, now that it's in excess.

It would be easy to fall into the trap of thinking that it is over. I almost gave into the feeling of, "oh my God, hospice means it's time to die." I have been fighting death so long that I let those feelings past and I have never sought sympathy from anyone.

I became very depressed the first day or two but only because the powers in hospice had to change my oxygen and medical equipment supplier that I have been with for over twenty years. That left me with a feeling of abandonment.

The new supplier will not provide the portable oxygen concentrator that I have been using the past two years and limit me to just four oxygen bottles a month. I have always remained active and that's enough for about two trips to town for shopping. I felt that they have just cut my legs off. I will surely die if I cannot remain active.

In recognition to my "emphysematic" loyalty with them for so many years, the company that supplied me with equipment gave me the portable machine. Now, I am free of the house anytime I wish. What good people. All the equipment I have bought over the years will go back to them and I have asked that it be distributed to those without insurance or money to buy what they need.

My condition worsens quickly now as time passes. Each time I think it can't get no worse, it does. I spend my time getting Jessie's personal affairs in order as she has not handled many things like paying bills and such. At any given time she could not tell you how much money she makes or has on hand. She has not had to cook for herself for at least twenty years and she is struggling with that process also.

If I wish to live any longer, the doctor has said that I need to slow down, and "stop doing things that get you running out of oxygen." After a few friendly quips back and forth we determined a course of action.

He said, "In view of your level of activity, you need to go home, sit down and shut up."

Of course, that brought immediate laughter out of all of us in the room.

If I wished to live any longer, these were the doctor's orders: medium doses of opiates, morphine and steroids. But what for? If I were a horse or a family pet, they would shoot me or put me to sleep.

January 2015, another year to enter into. What will this year bring me? Death for sure as I can only hope. I find the lack of thoughts of suicide comforting. I still think it's a good idea but I only realize that those thoughts do not come up any more. I presume my guardian angel is saying, "Enough already!" and refuses to hear any more.

It's ironic that hospice is provided to make death at home comfortable—and it does. But with the comfort provided, I realize I will go on for a lot longer. I'm comfortable, true, but still suffering, so that means they are prolonging life and the suffering that comes with it.

Don't get me wrong, I would not want to change what they are doing for me. These people at hospice are fantastic. In addition to paid staff, there are many volunteers that schedule time with me just to keep me company. Most all are spiritual believers and they do not let it bother them that I am an atheist. They are aware that I support their beliefs as another path to the same end.

The good people who are to publish my story have said to put it to rest, close it out, send it over and that's it. Like any good perfectionist, a project is never done but I have no choice.

EPILOGUE: PART 1

Regardless of all my oppressively solemn disclosures, I had a wonderful life. I befriended good love, but let it slip right out of my hands like a prized king salmon. As you have read, for decades, I served my country half-heartedly while at the same time serving my libido admirably.

Yes, sex took me from the pit to the palace. It snatched hold of the impressionable, horny lad and through lascivious conquests placed a well-deserved ill repute crown upon his head and sat him upon a thrown at the climax of his lecherous heartbreaking.

Fortunate for me, love gave me a second chance and I jumped to it, without considering the price. The tangled web of indiscretion I have woven cost me my sanity and health. Shadows of my past plagued me while deceased loved ones visit, harbingering my fate. Sickness entered my body long ago and has been a loyal companion ever since. Against my power, I am a man very much aware of my demise.

Unless you are dying, no one can possibly understand. If I were not dying, I am sure I would be just as apathetic. Still, the shadows come and so do visions whenever the hell they desire to check on me. It's like they are on watch or on reconnaissance for the One to show up. Dark objects effortlessly and gracefully dance into and out of my subconscious like the resplendent Northern Lights in an Alaskan sky. This is where my focus should be and not the life from which I have lived and soon will be departing. The debts of my life's lessons will be paid in full.

EPILOGUE: PART 2

My full life and all its unpleasantness has becomes too long, overpowering my usual slightly ecstatic demeanor.

All my mistakes have become too ingrained in my thoughts.

I strive for a perfect day just to escape.

Being the devout optimist, I can usually ignore unhappy memories and let a façade hide the shuddering effect of past indiscretions.

No more. I am tired of dodging the potholes before me.

My demise approaches. I have many regrets but they are all for the future.

I regret that I cannot plant a tree and watch it grow.

Maybe a short term garden will suffice but I find the physical effort impossible.

I wish longingly for a puppy but just as we bond she will wonder where I have gone, how sad.

I wonder if I will outlive my cat, I do not wish to.

I enjoy road trips as I know I can squeeze them in, they have a beginning and an end.

I'm glad my life wasn't that short.

Where has time gone?

The End

ABOUT THE AUTHOR

Arthur A. Jennings
August 5, 1943 –
May 20, 2015

Arthur Allen Jennings worked on his memoirs while in hospice care in Wasilla, Alaska. On a daily basis, he would struggle to make it his best while battling chronic pain, fatigue and pride. He made his transition on May 20, 2015. Long after his death, his memories and legacy lives on within these pages.

.....the possibility of a future when there is none. The contrast of the future as indicated by the covers travel to the end of day and the demise of the past as indicated by the young man that will never be again...